America's Best

Genealogy Resource Centers

Ron Bremer

2000

America's Best

Genealogy Resource Centers

William Dollarhide
and
Ronald A. Bremer

Heritage Quest
A Division of AGLL, Inc.
Bountiful, Utah
1999

Published by Heritage Quest,
a division of AGLL, Inc., Bountiful, Utah

Printed in the United States of America

2002   2001   2000   1999   5   4   3   2

ISBN 1-877677-90-6

Contents

Preface

This book identifies research facilities with genealogy collections at local, state, regional, and national levels. The top ten genealogy resource centers in the U.S. are listed first, followed by the locations of the best genealogy resource centers for each state. After the state listings, there are chapters for identifying the regional branches of the National Archives, and the vital statistics offices for each state.

Only a couple of guidebooks exist which identify genealogy resource centers in America. William Filby's *Directory of American Libraries with Genealogy or Local History Collections* was published in 1988 (Wilmington, DE: Scholarly Resources) and listed about 1,000 U.S. libraries who had responded to a survey. Although very useful in learning of genealogical collections in libraries, Filby's list omitted many important collections found in American archives, societies, as well as several national and regional facilities that did not return his survey. Genealogists are also familiar with *The Genealogist's Address Book* by Elizabeth Petty Bentley (3rd edition, 1996, Baltimore: Genealogical Publishing Co., Inc.). The *Address Book* provides a good listing of genealogical societies, libraries, and archives in the U.S., but it does not note the size or importance of the genealogy collections held by the various resource centers listed.

All of the genealogy resource centers identified in this book were surveyed in person. This was possible because the authors are two of the most traveled genealogists in America. Since 1972, Ron Bremer alone has traveled over a million miles and lectured at over 2,000 genealogical seminars in the U.S. and Canada. Since 1985, Bill Dollarhide has also traveled and lectured extensively. Together, the authors have personally visited and surveyed the collections held in over 3,000 genealogical and historical societies, libraries, and archives in all states.

While visiting each facility, the staff was asked about their special collections, surname folder files, genealogies, periodicals, county histories, and any other resource of value to genealogists. They were especially asked about any resource that made their library or archives unique, plus any compiled index or guide to a particular set of records. Based on these personal surveys and comparisons made between the various facilities, the list of 3,000 was condensed to an elite group of about 600 facilities, the very best genealogy resource centers in America.

In selecting the top ten genealogy resource centers, the first two were obvious choices, i.e., The Family History Library in Salt Lake City is clearly the largest and best facility of its kind in the world, and the prominence of the National Archives should not be disputed. However, all of the other top ten facilities could qualify as the number three choice. Therefore, the criteria followed was not to just select the largest facility but the one with the most unique genealogy collection for American researchers. For example, the DAR library was ranked slightly higher than the Ft. Wayne Library because much of the DAR Library's collection can be found no where else. While the Ft. Wayne Library's wonderful collection may be larger, it is not exclusive. Virtually everything in the Ft. Wayne Library can be found elsewhere.

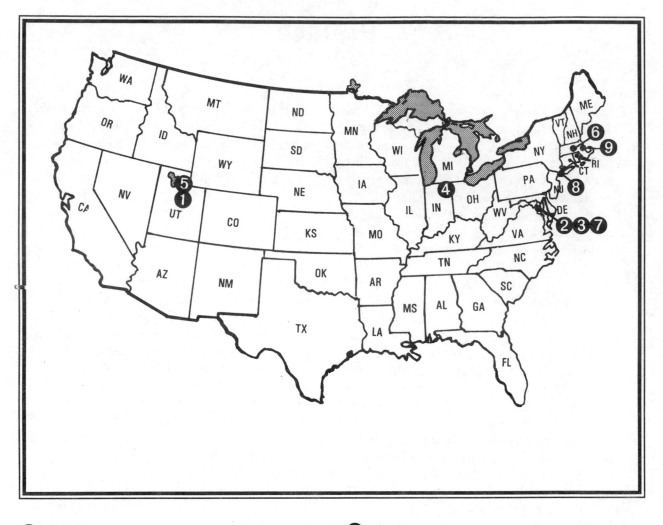

❶ Family History Library
Salt Lake City, Utah

❷ National Archives I & II
Washington, DC & College Park, MD

❸ Daughters of the American Revolution Library, Washington, DC

❹ Allen County Public Library
Fort Wayne, Indiana

❺ Heritage Quest
Bountiful, Utah

❻ American Antiquarian Society Library,
Worcester, Massachusetts

❼ Library of Congress
Washington, DC

❽ New York Public Library
New York City, New York

❾ New England Historic Genealogical Society, Boston, Massachusetts

❿ The Internet
The World Wide Web

The Top Ten
Genealogy Resource Centers
in America

The top ten genealogy resource centers in the U.S. are patronized by genealogical researchers from all over the country. Each of these important facilities are visited in great numbers by amateur genealogists in pursuit of evidence of their ancestors. Salt Lake City alone attracts nearly one million visitors each year to the Family History Library. It is not known how many genealogists visit the Washington D.C. area each year, but with three of the top ten facilities located there, the numbers are obviously very high. The rankings shown for the top facilities are based on the size and value of their collections to genealogists. The top ten resource centers are described below:

❶ **Family History Library**, 35 North West Temple, Salt Lake City, UT 84150. Phone: (801) 240-2331. Hours: 7:30 a.m. - 10:00 p.m., Tuesday through Saturday, and 7:30 a.m. - 5:00 p.m, Mondays. This is the largest genealogical library in the world, and the place where more research can be accomplished in one building than anywhere else in the country. With over two million rolls of microfilm, the collection contains births, deaths, marriages, deeds, and probates from county courthouses from most U.S. counties, as well as a large book collection and many historical documents on microfilm. The Family History Library's huge collection is beautifully organized through the use of their *Family Search* ™ system, a computerized card catalog which allows searches for any book or microfilm title by country, state, county, city, or town. Other finding tools are the FHL's *International Genealogical Index* ™ which is an index to over 225 million names extracted from parish and county records from countries all over the world, and the *Ancestral File* ™ which provides millions of names extracted from submitted pedigrees. In addition to a large selection of original U.S. state and county sources, the library has an excellent array of original records on microfilm from Mexico, Canada, England, Wales, Scotland, Ireland, Germany, and the Scandinavian countries. It has been said that a person with Mexican ancestry can accomplish more genealogy by visiting the Family History Library in Salt Lake City than by going to Mexico, since the library's microfilms of original parish christenings and other records covers virtually all regions of Mexico. The collection of microfilmed original documents relating to the British Isles is superior to any facility outside of Britain. Every serious genealogist will make a trip to Salt Lake City sooner or later.

❷ **National Archives and Records Administration, Archives I Reference Branch**, 8th Street and Pennsylvania Ave., N.W., Washington, DC 20408. Phone: (202) 501-5400 (public reference information). Internet website: www.nara.gov. Hours: Mon. and Wed., 8:45 am - 5:00 pm; Tues., Thurs, & Fri., 8:45am - 9:00pm; Sat. 8:45am - 4:45pm., and **Archives II Reference Branch**, 8601 Adelphi Road, College Park, MD 20740. Phone: (301) 713-7250 (textual reference). Hours: Monday & Wed. 8:45am - 5:00pm; Tues, Thurs, and Fri, 8:45am - 9:00pm; Sat. 8:45am - 4:45pm. These two facilities represent the main branches of the National Archives. The downtown Washington Archives I has 65,000 rolls of microfilm with importance for genealogical research, including federal censuses; ships' passenger arrival records; naturalization records; military and pension records; all public domain land entry files, including homesteads; and more. The Archives II facility at College Park, MD, has U.S. passport applications, District of Columbia Records, and records of the Cartographic and Architectural division. This latter division has the original topographic maps produced by the United States Geographic Survey beginning about 1888; drawings from patent applications; a large collection of aerial photographs of the U.S.; plus many other manuscripts. Together, these two facilities hold the greatest number of original historical documents available for genealogical research in America.

❸ **National Society of the Daughters of the American Revolution**, Genealogical Research Library, 1776 D Street, Washington, DC. Phone: (202) 879-3229. Hours: Monday - Friday 8:45 a.m. - 4 p.m., Sunday, 1 p.m.- 5 p.m. Non-DAR members pay a nominal fee for use of the library for research. The library is closed to non-DAR members during the annual conference in April each year. Since well before 1900, the many chapters of the DAR across the country have undertaken various projects to identify graves of Revolutionary Soldiers, index all burials in a particular cemetery, or extract and index county records such as birth, deaths, marriages, deeds, wills, and administrations. The results produced for most of these projects were typescripts, with an original copy sent to the DAR headquarters in Washington, DC. The DAR library today is the only place where many of these extracts and indexes can be found. Cemetery burials for thousands of U.S. cemeteries have been indexed, including a great many cemeteries that no longer exit. In addition, the genealogical book collection at the DAR Library is very large. The library's collection of federal census films is extensive, plus the library has virtually all printed census indexes. Add to that a large collection of lineages compiled by the many DAR members over the years, and this library is a genealogical treasure chest.

❹ **Allen County Public Library**, 900 Webster St., Fort Wayne, IN 46802. Phone: (219) 424-7241, ext. 2242. Internet address: **www.acpl.lib.in.us** The genealogy collection has 221,000 printed volumes plus 251,000 microform items. This library's collection shines in three areas: genealogical periodicals, printed county histories, and printed family histories. The Ft. Wayne library is the publisher of the Periodical Source Index (PERSI), an important name-subject index to articles in genealogical periodicals dating back to 1847. The library's collection of genealogical periodicals is unmatched by any library in the U.S. Its printed county history collection rivals that of the American Antiquarian Society, and the collection of 38,000 printed family histories may be unrivaled by any library in America. What really makes this library valuable is that its staff will conduct limited research through the mail for a fee. A researcher can submit a family name, place, and time period and the Ft. Wayne library staff will attempt to find a reference to that family.

❺ **Heritage Quest**, a division of AGLL, Inc., 593 W. 100 N., PO Box 329, Bountiful, UT 84011-0329. Toll-free phone: (800) 658-7755. This private membership library has a microfilm collection which surpasses any other private genealogy library in America in size. The collection is fully accessible by Heritage Quest members on loan with over 250,000 microfilm and microfiche titles related directly to genealogy subjects.

Virtually all National Archives microfilms are part of their collection, plus many more from local, regional, and state sources. Included in the collection are all federal censuses, 1790-1920, all soundex indexes on microfilm, plus many special censuses, such as agricultural, social statistics, mortality, and slave schedules, most U.S. Passenger lists, military records from the Revolutionary War times to 1900 and city, county, and state materials from all parts of the United States. In many cases, Heritage Quest has enhanced the images of National Archives census microfilm for readability, making their collection of census film superior to any other source. Heritage Quest is also America's largest supplier of genealogical products.

❻ **American Antiquarian Society Library**, 185 Salisbury St., Worcester, MA 01609-1634. Phone: (508) 755-5221. Hours: 9:00 a.m. - 5:00 a.m. Monday - Friday. Website: **gopher://mark.mwa.org/** This library is best known for its newspaper collection. For the U.S. alone, there are over 18,000 bound volumes of newspapers from 1704-1820 representing the single largest collection of extant newspapers for that period. In total, the library's documents are estimated to be 75% of all recorded American printing during its first two hundred years of existence. The huge holdings of this library rank in the top ten of all libraries in the U.S. for the categories of General American history, literature and bibliography; newspapers, periodicals and imprints to 1820; biography, genealogy and local history; almanacs, history and journalism; cookbooks, directories, book auction and dealers' catalogs; federal, state, and municipal documents, including New England town reports; college and school publications and amateur journalism; learned, historical and patriotic society publications; the literature of the Revolution; the War of 1812 and the westward movement; Negro literature, slavery, Civil War and reconstruction; American literature including early poetry, fiction and drama and modern first editions; children's literature and textbooks, the most extensive collection of the writings of the Mather family, their manuscripts, private library, family portraits; Bibles, hymnology, song books, and sheet music; early broadsides and broadside poetry and ballads; early maps, caricatures, copper-plates, lithographs, mezzotints and woodcuts, including the largest collection of American bookplates; stereoscopic and other photographic views and portraits; and manuscripts.

❼ Library of Congress, Local History and Genealogy Room, Thomas Jefferson Building, 101 Independence Ave. S.E., Washington, DC 20540. Phone: (202) 707-6400. Hours: 8:30 a.m. - 9:30 p.m., Monday, Wednesday, Thursday; and 8:30 a.m. - 5 p.m., Tuesday, Friday, and Saturday. The Local History and Genealogy room is located on the ground floor. This facility is best for its guides and indexes, but the main Library of Congress electronic card catalog is the key to locating book titles on any subject — the resources in this library are unmatched by any other library in the world. A free on-line catalog

search is available on the Internet at **http://www.loc.gov/** and gives anyone access to the huge collection of books, manuscripts, the largest collection of maps in the world, and many historical documents. In addition, the library's photo-duplication service supplies photocopies of items located in the Library's collections if there are no copyright restrictions. This is the method to first search for a particular title, then have copies made. This copying service is a cost recovery operation, and assesses a non-refundable $10.00 advance payment for each order to cover identifying and assembling material to be copied. The advance payment also covers photocopying of short articles of up to 25 exposures and serves as partial payment for larger orders. Cost quotations will be provided for orders exceeding 25 exposures. Photocopy rates are $.50 per exposure (with one exposure normally including two pages). Payments may be made by MasterCard or Visa, an international money order, or a check drawn on a US bank. Requests should be directed to the Library of Congress, Photo-duplication Service, Washington, D.C. 20540-4570.

❽ The New York Public Library, 5th Avenue and 42nd Street, New York City, NY 10018. Phone: (212) 869-8089. The U.S. History, Local History & Genealogy Division is located in the New York Public Library's Center for the Humanities. The Division collects materials documenting American History on the national, state, and local level, genealogy, heraldry, personal and family names, and flags. Holdings in United States town, city, county, and state histories are national in scope. Genealogical materials are international in scope. Visual resources include photographic and negative collections, primarily of New York City views, and over 300,000 postcards documenting United States local views. A local history ephemera collection of pamphlets, leaflets, etc., provides primary study materials for the cultural, social, and religious history of the United States. The Division also collects political campaign ephemera, including broadsides, pamphlets, and candidate position papers. Vertical files and genealogical charts further enhance the Division's holdings.

The collection includes the printed library catalogs, handbooks and guides; New York City vital records indexes; census records; U.S. military sources; a New York DAR records repository; an extensive collection of Loyalist claim records; Irish sources; regional records; newspapers and indexes; city and telephone directories; family histories, periodicals, photographic collections and genealogical sources of the LDS Church. Of interest to the New York region, the library has the Index (Soundex) to Naturalization Petitions, 1792-1906 for New York, Kings, Queens, and Richmond Counties; and the alphabetical index to petitions for naturalization of the U.S. District Court for the Eastern District of New York, 1865-1957.

Access to the holdings of the New York Public Library is made convenient through the use of **CATNYP** (**CAT**alog of the **N**ew **Y**ork **P**ublic Library), available through the internet. However, the on-line catalog only includes materials cataloged since 1972. (A search of CATNYP for the word "genealogy" found 12,211 entries) . The 800 volume *Dictionary Catalog of The Research Libraries, 1911-1972*, published by G.K. Hall is a complete catalog listing of more than one million non-circulating titles held by the New York Public Library.

The Center for the Humanities map division, located on the 1st floor, is a world class collection of maps and enhances the overall usefulness of the genealogy collection. Maps can be retrieved by subject, place, or title.

❾ **New England Historic Genealogical Society Library**, 101 Newbury St., Boston, MA 02116-3087. Phone: (617) 536-5740. As a repository for New England materials of genealogical interest, there is no better facility. But this private library also contains materials for virtually every state, a huge Canadian collection, and many materials related to the British Isles, Ireland, and continental Europe. The library features a book rental program for its members and has one of the largest manuscript genealogies collections in the world, containing diaries and letters; account books and business papers; church and town records; sermons, maps, wills, deeds; and unpublished New England genealogies. The unpublished manuscripts, genealogies, and books are contained on over 5,280 lineal feet of shelf space (a full mile of reference materials). Since the 1850s, the papers of many of the leading genealogists in America have been kept here, with detailed genealogies for many thousands of families. For anyone with New England ancestors, a membership in this organization is a must.

❿ The Internet. The *World Wide Web* is an interface system which allows a computer user to access millions of databases stored on private and public computers all over the world, called the *Internet*. For genealogists, the Internet has become an important place for locating databases valuable for genealogical research. This is true because a large number of libraries and archives can be found. The Internet has become one of the most important genealogy resource centers in America. Although it has no single location or address, as a whole, the resources of the Internet exceed virtually any single resource center in size. Currently, the Internet is best for locating databases available for finding people (dead or alive); on-line searching of name lists, indexes, and library catalogs; downloading software for various uses; education and training in specific areas of historical research; help in travel, booking airline flights, printing maps for a specific region, or planning genealogy trips; aids in translating languages; finding places, dates, and subjects of genealogy conferences, seminars and classes; locating addresses and phone numbers for historical societies, genealogical societies, libraries, or archives anywhere in the world; direct purchases of genealogical products and services from vendors of books, charts, or software; contacting other genealogists with a common interest; and many other services worldwide. The Internet is not yet the best

place to find copies of actual court records, such as deed records, birth and death records, or scanned images of historical documents. The Internet is becoming, however, the best place to learn what type of documents with genealogical value may exist in a particular library or archives. Of interest to genealogists are some powerful databases for locating a wide range of published and unpublished materials worldwide. Here are three examples of important Internet databases for which a subscription fee is required:

○ **The On-line Computer Library Center (OCLC).** This is the largest bibliographic database in the world. The OCLC includes the National Union Catalog of Manuscript Collections (NUCMC), a comprehensive index to original manuscripts and unpublished documents held in libraries and archives worldwide. The OCLC's "First Search" feature allows for system-wide searching for an author, title, or subject. This database requires a user to purchase a subscription. It was designed for the use of librarians in public and private libraries to search catalog information in libraries and archives anywhere in the world. Genealogists can usually access this database at a local library, or an individual membership can be purchased.

○ **Research Library Information Network (RLIN).** This is another bibliographic database used primarily by librarians to determine the existence of manuscripts located in major repositories. A subscription is required to use this database, but it is available to patrons of many public and private libraries.

○ **The Center for Research Libraries (CRL)**. This library is mainly for scholarly access to research materials rarely found in the United States. The collection contains over 3.6 million volumes and 1.1 million microforms. Within the collection are 6,100 foreign newspapers from 167 different countries in 107 languages, all on microfilm. CRL is particulary valuable for accessing historical collections found in Slavic and East European libraries and archives. Access to CRL's bibliographic database is usually done through university libraries, but with the database now accessible on the Internet (through RLIN), a subscriber can learn of unique sources for genealogical research in many foreign resources centers.

Some examples of free databases available on the Internet are:

○ **MedAccess**. This is a free database where anyone can locate a Vital Statistics Office for any state, along with the mailing address, cost of birth, death, or marriage certificates, and the dates when the records begin.

○ **Genealogy Resource Lists**. Several free databases allow a researcher to find lists of World Wide Web sites relating to genealogy. Examples: *Cyndi's List of Genealogy Sites on the Internet*; *Roots Web,* and the *US GenWeb*. As more genealogical databases come on-line, these lookup lists are updated and become valuable to see what is available on the Internet.

○ **Library Catalog Searches.** Thousands of libraries and archives have complete card catalog access on the Internet. Anyone can access these free electronic card catalogs and conduct a search by title, author's name, or subject. Some notable facilities with catalog search capabilities are the Library of Congress, the Allen County Public Library, the American Antiquarian Society, and the Library of Virginia.

○ **Manuscript Society Information Exchange Database.** As an example of powerful databases on the Internet, this website is one where privately held manuscripts are identified. The database contains a broad range of material national and international in scope. The manuscripts identified are held not by libraries or archives, but by private individuals throughout the United States. The database identifies the holders of the manuscripts and their locations. Many documents are authored by historical figures and personalities, such as Edwin Booth, Queen Isabella I, Sam Houston, Joannes Brahms, Catherine de Medicis, Mark Twain, and Robert E. Lee. United States presidents and their wives are well represented. The database can be searched for documents by an individual or about an individual. The database is also accessible by subject. The database is maintained by the Department of Archives and Manuscripts at Arizona State University and the Manuscript Society.

State and Regional
Genealogy Resource Centers

The best place to find references to your ancestors may be at a local library, archives, or genealogical society. Since genealogical references are most often found near the place where a person lived, the best resources may be in the county and state records that exist today. These local records may include births, deaths, marriages, deeds, probates, land and tax records, and many others. The local records are the ones that provide direct evidence of a person's life, and often the desired proof of relationships. These local records include primary records, or primary records on microfilm. Hence, they are records of great value to genealogists. But local collections also include secondary records compiled by a researcher living in the local region, and these secondary sources can be very valuable to genealogists as well. Records collected by genealogical societies, historical societies; local and college libraries; and local archives and museums may be specific to a small region of the U.S. and not readily available elsewhere.

For example, most of the records generated at a local courthouse are still in the courthouse office that originated them. In some states, some of the early courthouse records have been moved to a state facility, such as a state archives. A genealogical researcher needs to know where the local courthouse records are kept today, and in what form they may be available for research, either in original form or in the form of microfilm.

The libraries and archives shown for each state are listed because of their significance to genealogists. The first facility listed for each state has the largest and most important collection for that state. In some states, the best facility for genealogical research may be a regional facility outside of that state. After the first facility listed, as many as ten or more facilities are shown for each state. As a group, these facilities represent the best genealogy resource centers in a state; but except for the first facility listed, they are not shown in any ranked order.

A locator map for each state shows the main highways and identifies the location of the cities where the best genealogy resource centers are located. The maps can be used as a guide to follow in visiting the resource facilities. All maps were hand drawn by William Dollarhide specifically for this publication.

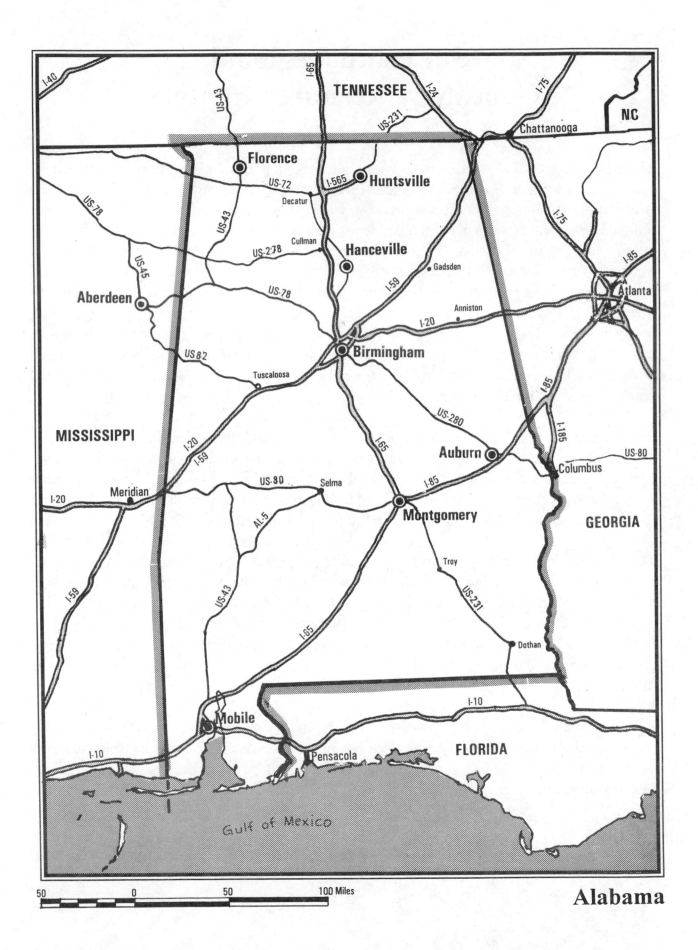

Alabama

Alabama

Department of Archives and History, 624 Washington Ave., Montgomery AL 36130-0100. Phone: (334) 242-4435. Every county represented with local records, marriages, deeds, etc. This is the starting place for research in Alabama territorial and state records. As an example of what can be found for every county, the original records for Baldwin County, Alabama are as follows: Will records, 1809-1909; Direct Index to Probate records, 1810-1925; Direct Index to Deeds, 1905-1935; Reverse Index to Deeds, 1810-1911; Deed Records, 1809-1901; General Index to Orphans Court and Probate Court records, 1820-1930; Orphans Court records, 1822-1854; Probate Court records, 1855-1929; Orphans Court minutes, 1822-1856; Probate Court minutes, 1850-1928; Tax Assessor's records of personal property, 1849 Vital Records; and Newspapers. All other Alabama counties have a similar array of records.

Huntsville-Madison County Public Library, 915 Monroe Street, Huntsville, AL 35801. Phone: (205) 532-5940. The best genealogical collection for Alabama families and a starting point in all time periods of Alabama. In addition to Alabama sources, there is a good array of references for the southern states.

Davis Library, Samford University, 800 Lakeshore Dr., Birmingham, AL 35229-0001. Phone: (205) 870-2846. One of the best genealogy resource centers in the south. This library houses original and secondary genealogical and historical sources primarily for Alabama and the Southeast; the Irish Historical Collection focusing primarily on counties Cork and Kerry; manuscripts of local and family history; Baptist records; maps; local historical and genealogical periodicals; and newspapers.

Mobile Public Library, 701 Government St., Mobile, AL. 36602-1449. Phone: (334) 208-7073. A very good genealogy department in its own building.

Birmingham Public Library, 2100 Park Place, Birmingham, AL 35203. Phone: (205) 226-3600. A good collection of books, periodicals, maps, and family folders.

Evans Memorial Library, 105 N. Long Street; Aberdeen, MS 39730. Phone: (601)369-4601. This is an outstanding regional library for the Deep South including Alabama oral histories, church records, newspapers, scrapbooks, maps, military records, Chickasaw tribe, folklore, travel, Afro-Americans, fraternal histories, manuscripts, and photographs.

Mobile Municipal Archives, PO Box 1827, Mobile, AL 36633-1827. Phone: (334) 208-7740. Archives includes records of early Alabama settlers, Spanish, French, Anglos, and more. This is a premier library for references to the Gulf Coast areas from Louisiana to Florida.

Wallace State Community College Library, PO Box 2000, Hanceville, AL 35077-2000. Phone: (205) 352-6403. Small college with a good library. The genealogy section is growing.

Draughon Library, Auburn University, Auburn, AL 36849-5606. Phone: (334) 844-4500. The holdings include family histories, books, passenger lists, dictionaries of names, and more.

Florence-Lauderdale Public Library, 218 N. Wood Ave., Florence, AL 35630. Phone: (205) 764-6563. Very good Civil War, genealogy, and local history collections.

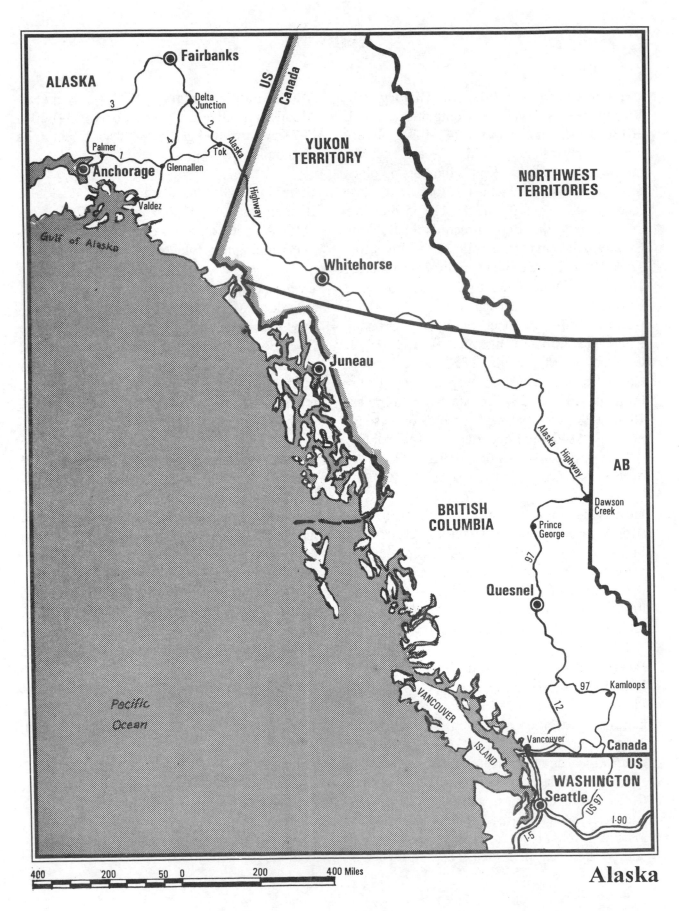

Alaska

Alaska

Suzzallo Library, University of Washington, Seattle, WA 98195-0001. Phone: (206) 543-1760. The Pacific Northwest and Alaska coverage for historical materials is outstanding. This library may have more materials relating to Alaska than any library or archives in Alaska.

Alaska Historical Library, State Office Building, PO Box 110571, Juneau, AK 99811-0571. Phone: (907) 465-2925. Alaskana, Alaska-Arctic research, marine history, Russian-American research, photographs, and more.

Alaska State Library, State Office Bldg., PO Box 110571 Juneau, Alaska 99811-0571. Phone: (907) 465-2910. A good historical collection of early Alaska settlers.

Anchorage Municipal Library, 3600 Denali, Anchorage, AK 99503-6093. Phone: (907) 261-2975. Alaska history, genealogies, and oral histories.

University of Alaska Library, 3211 Providence Dr., Anchorage, AK 99508. Phone: (907) 786-1825. Alaska Natives, Alaskana, and some Alaska genealogy.

Alaska Archives and Records Management Services, 141 Willoughby Ave., Juneau, AK 99801-1720. Phone: (907) 465-2275. Alaska government, history, and culture.

Rasmuson Library, University of Alaska, PO Box 756808, Fairbanks, AK 99775-6808. Phone: (907) 474-7224. Alaska and the Polar region, and oral histories of Alaska pioneers. An index to the oral histories on audio tapes is available on the Internet.

Alaskana Collection and Archives, 4101 University Dr., Anchorage, AK 99508. Phone: (907) 561-1265. Primary source of those who came north to Alaska: Early gold miners, cannery workers, teachers, ministers, and settlers.

Libraries and Archives Branch, (Territorial Archives), PO box 2703, Whitehorse, YT Y1A 2C6 Canada. Phone: (403) 667-5309. Territorial archive center with name lists to most of the early miners to Yukon Territory. Most miners passed through Alaska to get to Dawson, Yukon Territory.

Quesnel and District Museum, 405 Barlow Ave., Quesnel, BC B2J 2C3. Phone: (250) 992-9580 (summers). Most extensive archives with records of the great Alaska-Yukon gold rush, mostly during the 1890s, but covering the period 1850-1950. Indexes of names of people who came to the gold fields, plus manuscripts, newspaper notices, claims, lists of groups. Many people who came through Alaska to the gold fields can be found here.

Klondike Gold Rush National Historical Park, 117 S. Main St., Seattle, WA 98104. Phone: (206) 553-7220. Celebrates Seattle's role as the jumping off point for the Klondike. Includes Alaskan diaries, letters, and more.

National Archives, Pacific Alaska Region, (Anchorage), 654 W. 3rd Ave., Anchorage, AK 99501. Phone: (907) 271-2441. The reading room has all microfilm for U.S. federal censuses 1790-1920 for all states, all soundex indexes, and virtually all printed indexes to statewide censuses. The archives has many historical records dating from about 1867.

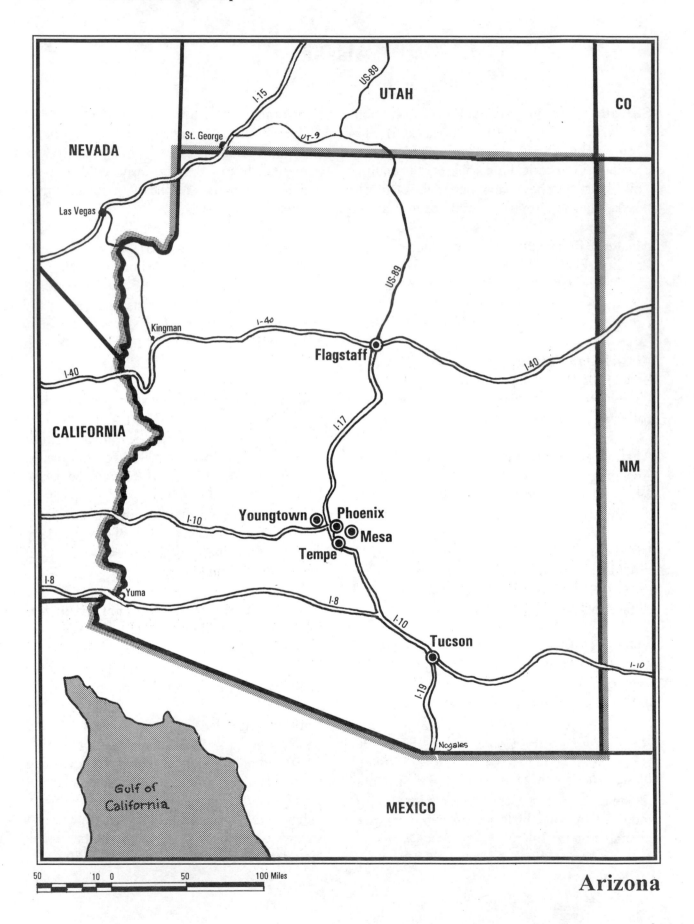

Arizona

Arizona

Arizona State Library, Genealogy Section, State Capitol, 1700 W. Washington St., Phoenix, AZ 85007. Phone: (602) 542-4121. The starting place for Arizona research. Census film, books, periodicals, and more. Primarily a book library, but a good one.

Mesa Family History Center, The Church of Jesus Christ of Latter-day Saints, 41 S. Hobson, Mesa, AZ 85204. Phone: (602) 964-1200. A good selection of genealogy books, covering the entire U.S. and a great collection of federal census film. This is one of the largest Family History Centers in America. Open to the public.

Arizona State University Library, Special Collections, Carl Hayden Archives, PO Box 871006, Arizona State University, Tempe, AZ 85287-1006. Phone: (602) 965-3950. For early Arizona families, this is a good place to look.

University of Arizona Library, Special Collections, PO Box 210055, Tucson, AZ 85721-0055. Phone: (520) 621-6423. Southwestern American history and Borderlands collection.

Arizona Historical Society Library, 949 E. 2nd St., Tucson, AZ 85719. Phone: (520) 628-5775. Early Arizona Collection, early Mexican records, Colorado River subjects, and maps. This is a very good genealogy resource center, operated by a one of the most active genealogical societies in the country.

Cline Library, Northern Arizona University, CU Box 6022, Flagstaff, AZ 86011-6022. Phone: (520) 523-2171. Arizona history, Arizona photographs, archives, and oral histories.

Maricopa County Library, 17811 N. 32nd St., Phoenix, AZ 85032. Phone: (602) 506-2957. The Southwest Collection has Arizona histories, genealogies, family folders, and more.

Phoenix Public Library, 1221 N. Central, Phoenix, AZ 85004. Phone: (602) 262-4636. Arizona history collection, and a good collection for genealogical research.

Tucson Public Library, 101 N. Stone Ave., PO Box 27470, Tucson, AZ 85726-7470. Phone: (520) 791-4393. Arizona Collection, Southern Arizona Genealogical Society collection is located here.

Sun Cities Genealogical Society Library, 11116 California, Youngtown, AZ 85363. Phone: (602) 933-4945. This is a very active genealogical group with a small, but very good library. There is probably more genealogical references for outside Arizona, due to a retirement community depositing many genealogies from all over the U.S.

Bancroft Library, University of California, Berkeley, CA 94720. Phone: (415) 642-3781. The "Bancroft Collection" is outstanding for early settlers, early trails, stagecoaches, miners, histories, etc. This library may have more historical material about Arizona than any library in Arizona.

Southwest Museum, Braun Research Library, 234 Museum Dr., PO Box 41558, Highland Park, CA 90041-0558. Phone: (213) 221-2164. This library contains the Monk Library of Arizoniana, California and Arizona history, and early records of Southwestern Indians.

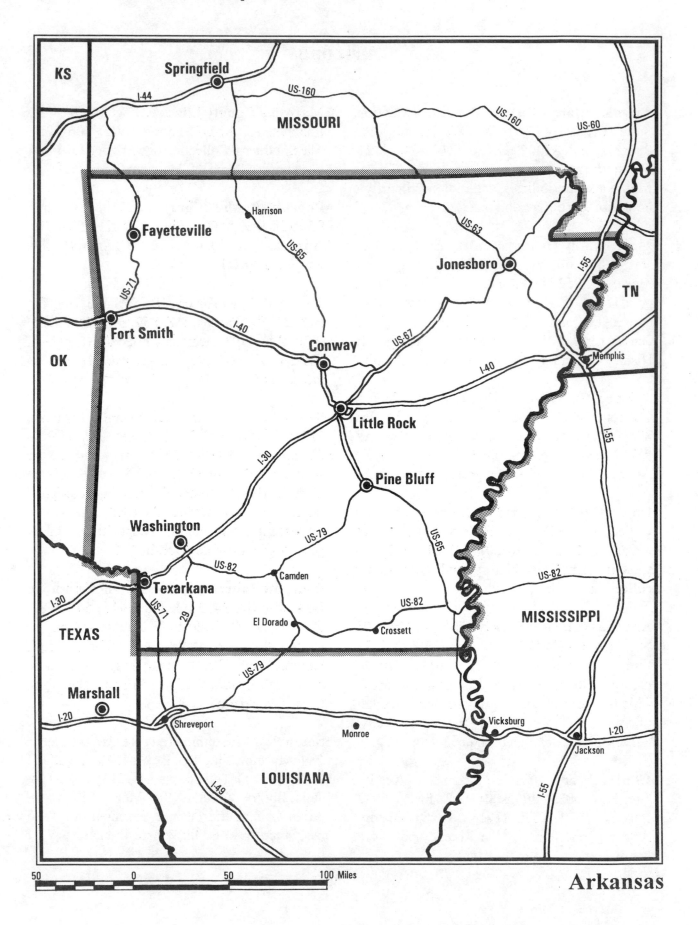

Arkansas

Arkansas

Arkansas State History Commission Archives, One Capitol Mall, Little Rock, AR 72201. Phone: (501) 682-6900. A collection of original and microfilmed records for all county vital records, deeds, probates, etc., as well as many family histories and many other genealogical records. This is a one-stop place for research in Arkansas, plus it has numerous references to the entire South, Civil War, Folklore, Ozarks, Black History, and Religions — and a great staff who will help people find their ancestors.

Arkansas State Library, 1 Capitol Mall, Little Rock, AR 72201. Phone: (501) 682-1527. Arkansiana collection, local and state histories, and genealogy. Book collection is probably the best in the state.

University of Arkansas Library, Special Collections, Fayetteville, AR 72701. Phone: (501)575-8444. County records, newspapers, manuscripts, church records, Arkansas Collection, Ozarks history, state history, and genealogy.

Southwest Arkansas Regional Archives (SARA), PO Box 134, Washington, AR 71862. Phone: (870) 983-2633. Although its speciality is Southwest Arkansas, this facility has references that can solve some of the hardest parts of research in Arkansas — finding those settlers who came through Arkansas from Kentucky, Tennessee, and Georgia, enroute to Texas. Many early records not at Little Rock are here for early Arkansas people.

Fort Smith Public Library, 61 S. 8th St., Fort Smith, AR 72901-2480. Phone: (501) 783-0229. Local and state history and genealogy references in the "Arkansas Collection".

Ozarks Regional Library, 217 E. Dickson St., Fayetteville, AR 72701. Phone: (501) 442-6253. Genealogy collection is quite good for early Arkansas people.

Texarkana Public Library, 600 W. 3rd St., Texarkana, TX 75501. Phone: (214) 794-2149. Outstanding Texas and Arkansas local history and genealogy collection.

Harrison County Historical Museum, Hughes Research Center Library, Marshall, TX 75670. Phone: (903) 938-2680. Marshall, Texas was a confederate center during the Civil War. Many early Arkansas records can be found here for the period right after the war.

Pine Bluff - Jefferson County Library, 200 E. 8th Ave., Pine Bluff, AR 71601. Phone: (870) 534-4802. Nice genealogy room. Records for the whole state. Indexes, surname folders, genealogies, and more.

Ozarks Genealogical Society Library, PO Box 3494, Springfield, MO 65804. Genealogies of Arkansas Ozarks families, plus newspapers, family folders, obituaries, cemeteries, and more.

Craighead County - Jonesboro Public Library, 315 W. Oak, Jonesboro, AR 72401. Phone: (870) 935-5133. Good genealogy section, with a good Arkansas collection. Family folders, indexes, periodicals, books, microfilm, and more.

Torreyson Library, University of Central Arkansas, 201 Donaghey Ave., Conway, AR 72032. Phone: (501) 450-3129. This library has a solid genealogy collection with many references to Arkansas.

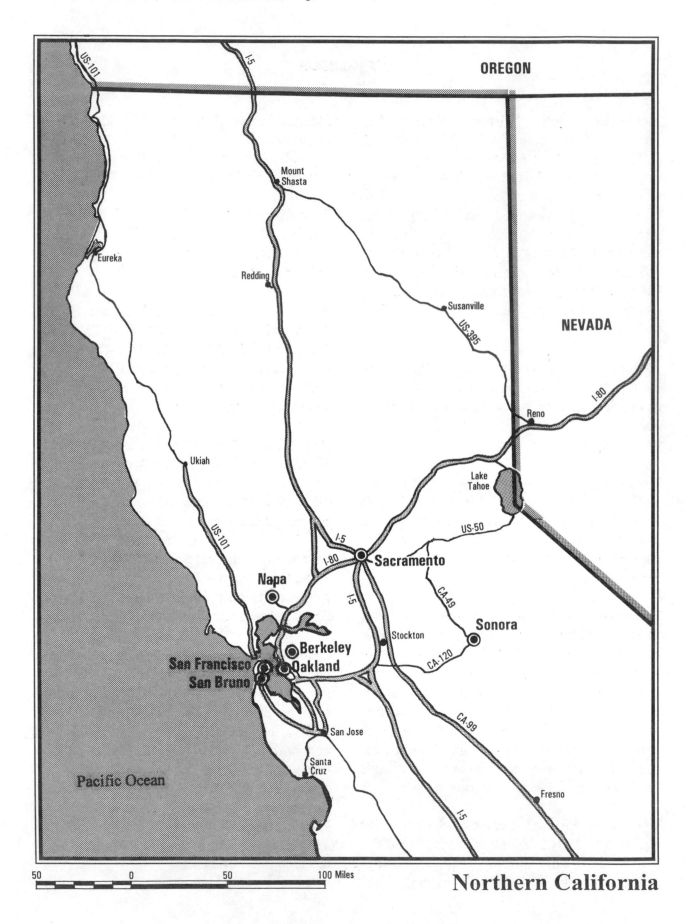

Northern California

Northern California

Bancroft Library, University of California, Berkeley, CA 94720. Phone: (415) 642-3781. The "Bancroft Collection" is outstanding for early settlers, early trails, stagecoaches, miners, histories, etc. This library has more historical material about Western North America than any other facility in the U.S.

California State Library, 914 Capitol Mall, PO Box 942837, Sacramento, CA 94327-0001. Phone: (916) 654-0176. Great newspaper collection for California cities. Largest genealogical index in the state. Statewide birth and death records.

Sutro Library, Branch of California State Library, 480 Winston Dr., San Francisco, CA 94132. Phone: (415) 731-4477. An excellent genealogy and local history collection. *The* place for genealogical research in northern California. An excellent collection of census film, books, and periodicals, for most states.

Oakland Family History Library, 4766 Lincoln Ave., Oakland, CA 94602. Phone: (510) 531-3905. Census film, books, genealogies, and more.

National Archives, Pacific Region (San Francisco), 1000 Commodore Dr., San Bruno, CA 94066. Phone: (650) 876- All U.S. federal censuses, 1790-1920, plus all soundex indexes (on microfilm), and all printed statewide census indexes.

California Genealogical Society Library, 300 Brannan St., PO Box 77105, San Francisco, CA 94107-0105. Phone: (415) 777-9936. Genealogy collection for California and the entire country.

California Historical Society Library, 2099 Pacific Ave., San Francisco, CA 94109-2235. Phone: (415) 357-1848. Manuscript and archives collection, California histories, imprints, county and municipal histories, early California voyages, ethnic histories, Gold Rush, Mexican War, rare books, women in California, and more.

Society of California Pioneers Library, PO Box 191850, San Francisco, CA 94119. Phone: (415) 957-1849. Diaries, papers, local histories, and directories from 1850. California history from the earliest explorers to 1900.

Napa Valley Genealogical & Historical Society Library, PO Box 4654, Napa, CA 94559. Phone: (707) 252--2252. Great genealogy collection, heavy on New England materials.

State Land Commission, Boundary Section Map & Book Center, 100 Howe Ave., Suite 100 South, Sacramento, CA 95825. Phone: (916) 574-1900. California land surveys, titles, property boundaries, school lands, tide lands mapping, state land Township plats, Mexican land grants in California, public land surveys, and Rancho land grants.

Tuolumne County Genealogical Society Library, 158 W. Bradford St., PO Box 3956, Sonora, CA 95370. Located in the heart of the California gold rush district, this society's library is housed in the county museum and shared with the county historical society. A unique index to the early miners and setters of California can be found here, called the "Gone West Index".

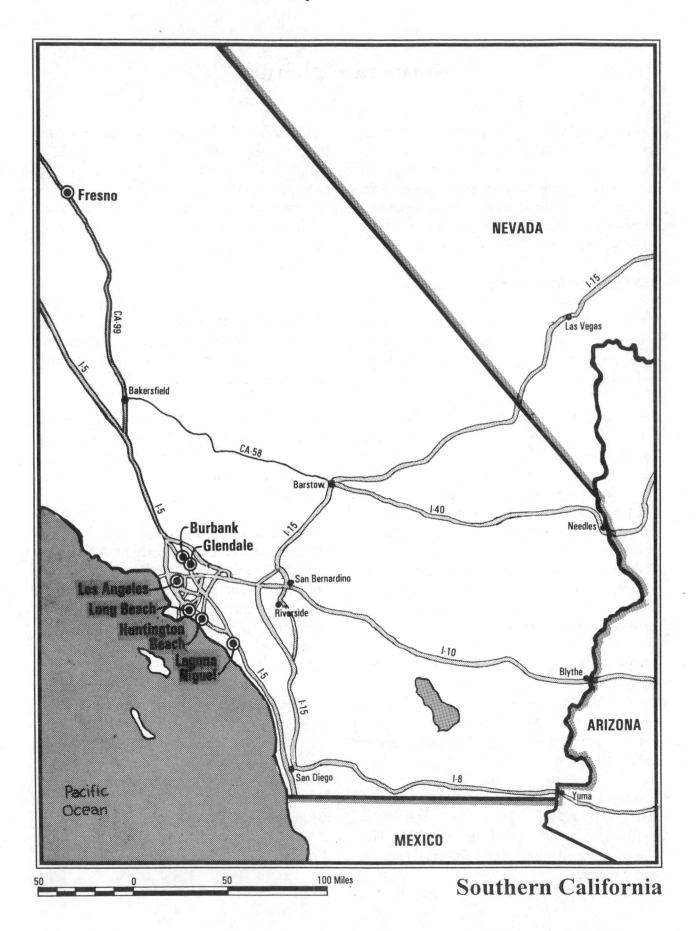

Southern California

Southern California

Los Angeles Public Library, History and Genealogy Department, 630 W. Fifth St., Los Angeles, CA 90071-2097. Phone: (213) 612-3200. Excellent biographical indexes. Great genealogy collection. *The* place for research in Southern California.

Los Angeles Family History Center, The Church of Jesus Christ of Latter-day Saints, 10741 Santa Monica Blvd., Los Angeles, CA 90025. Phone: (310) 474-9990. One of the largest LDS Family History Centers in America. Great collection of census film, genealogies, histories, and more.

Natural History Museum of Los Angeles County, Research Library, 900 Exposition Blvd., Los Angeles, CA 90007. Phone: (213) 763-3466. California Indians, pre-1900 So. Calif. Newspapers, So. Calif. & Los Angeles history, Spanish and Mexican eras, seafarers.

National Archives, Pacific Region (Laguna Niguel), 24000 Avilla Rd., first floor, east entrance, Laguna Niguel, CA 92677-3405. Phone: (714) 643-4241. All microfilm for U.S. federal censuses, 1790-1920 plus all soundex and printed census indexes.

Southern California Genealogical Society Library, 417 Irving Dr., Burbank, CA 91504-2408. Phone: (818) 843-7247. A good genealogical collection for California and the rest of the country.

Immigrant Genealogical Society Library, 1310-B W. Magnolia Blvd., Burbank, CA 91510. Phone: (818) 848-3122. Collection is mostly for German immigrants. More German records than any other U.S. library except the Family History Library in Salt Lake.

Fresno City and County Historical Society Archives, PO Box 2029, Fresno, CA 93718. Phone: (209) 441-0862. Indexes to locate early farmers in the great Central Valley can be found here, with many biographies, plus a strong genealogy collection. You must make an appointment to visit and use this facility.

Long Beach Public Library, 101 Pacific Ave., Long Beach, CA 90802-4482. Phone: (562) 570-7500. California history and Rancho period, computer indexes to statewide records, such as Great Registers, miners, early settlers, and Mexican era.

Huntington Beach Library, Information and Cultural Resource Center, 7111 Talbot Ave. Huntington Beach, CA 92648. Phone: (714) 842-4481. Genealogy collection of the Orange County Genealogical Society. Collection includes books, periodicals, and microfilm.

County of Los Angeles Public Library, 7400 E. Imperial Highway, PO Box 7011, Los Angeles, CA 90241-7011. Phone: (562) 940-8462. Californiana, Hispanic studies, and more.

Sons of the Revolution Library, 600 S. Central Ave., Glendale, CA 91204. Phone: (818) 240-1775. American military records, genealogies, local histories, vital records, with coverage for the entire U.S., plus some Canada and Britain.

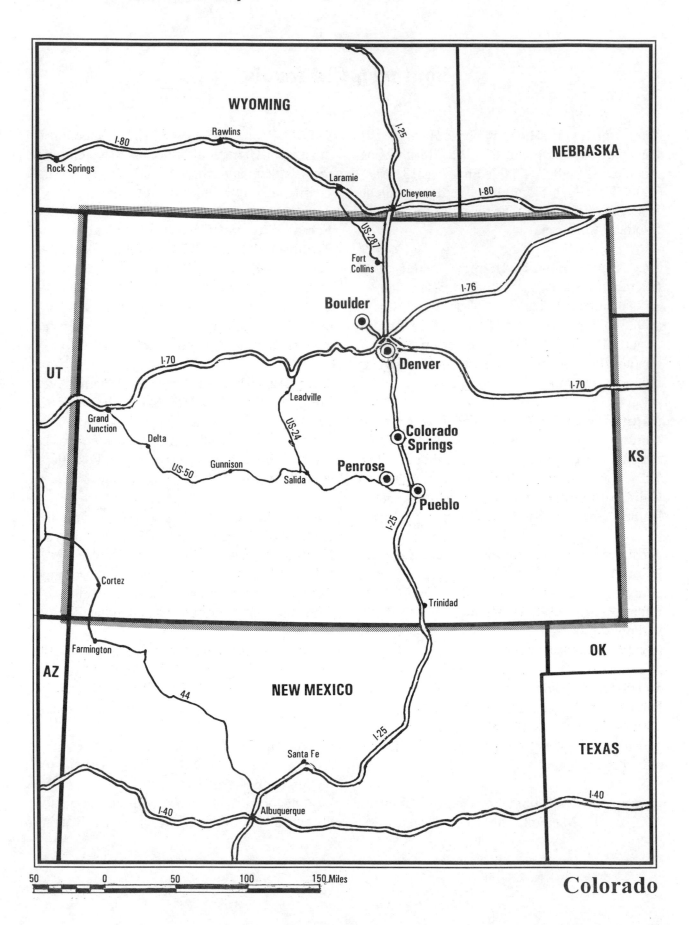

Colorado

Colorado

Colorado State Archives. 1313 Sherman St., Room 1B-20, Denver, CO 80203. Phone: (303) 866-2358. Territorial, early statehood, and county records statewide, military, and more. This is the place for Colorado genealogical research.

Colorado Historical Society, Stephen H. Hart Library, 1300 Broadway, Denver, CO 80203. Phone: (303) 866-2305. Wagon trains, stage lines, cowboys, cattle trails, early lawmen, outlaws, early land grants, homesteaders, and miners.

Colorado State Library, 201 E. Colfax, Denver, CO 80203-1799. Phone: (303) 866-6900. Colorado histories, biographies, county and town histories, and genealogies.

Bancroft Library, University of California, Berkeley, CA 94720. Phone: (415) 642-3781. The "Bancroft Collection" is outstanding for early settlers, early trails, stagecoaches, miners, histories, etc. This library has many historical documents relating to early Colorado.

Norland Library, University of Colorado, Box 184, Boulder, CO 80309-0184. Phone: (303) 492-7521. Western Historical Collection, news-papers, books, diaries, journals, early settlers, farmers, miners, and shepherds.

Denver Public Library, 10 W. 14th Ave. Parkway, Denver, CO 80204. Phone: (303) 640-6200. Western History/Genealogy Department. A very good Colorado collection.

National Archives, Rocky Mountain Region, Denver Federal Center, Building 48, Denver, CO 80225. Phone: (303) 236-0804. All microfilm for U.S. federal censuses, 1790-1920 plus all soundex indexes and virtually all printed statewide census indexes. This regional archives has federal records from Colorado, Montana, New Mexico, North Dakota, South Dakota, Utah, and Wyoming.

Carnegie Library, branch of Boulder Public Library, 1125 Pine, Boulder, CO 80302. Phone: (303) 441-3110. Colorado historical documents collection, Boulder city and county histories, historical photographs collections, and a good genealogy collection.

Tutt Library, Colorado College, 1021 N. Cascade Ave., Colorado Springs, CO 80903. Phone: (719) 389-6658. Colorado newspapers, books, pamphlets, imprints, clippings and manuscripts relating to development of Colorado Springs, historical manuscripts, and Western Americana.

Penrose Public Library, Pikes Peak Library District, 20 N. Cascade Ave., Colorado Springs, CO 80903. Phone: (719) 531-6333. Census, DAR lineage books, PA Archives, and more. A good basic collection for genealogical research.

Pueblo County Historical Society Library, 217 Grand Ave., Pueblo, CO 81003. Phone: (719) 543-6772. Early Colorado histories, biographies, oral histories, and newspapers.

Friend Library, 1448 Q St., Penrose, CO 81240-9689. Phone: (719) 372-6726. A private collection available by appointment only. If your ancestor came to Colorado 1850-1890, whether a settler, robber, convict, or miner, you will probably find a reference to him in this library.

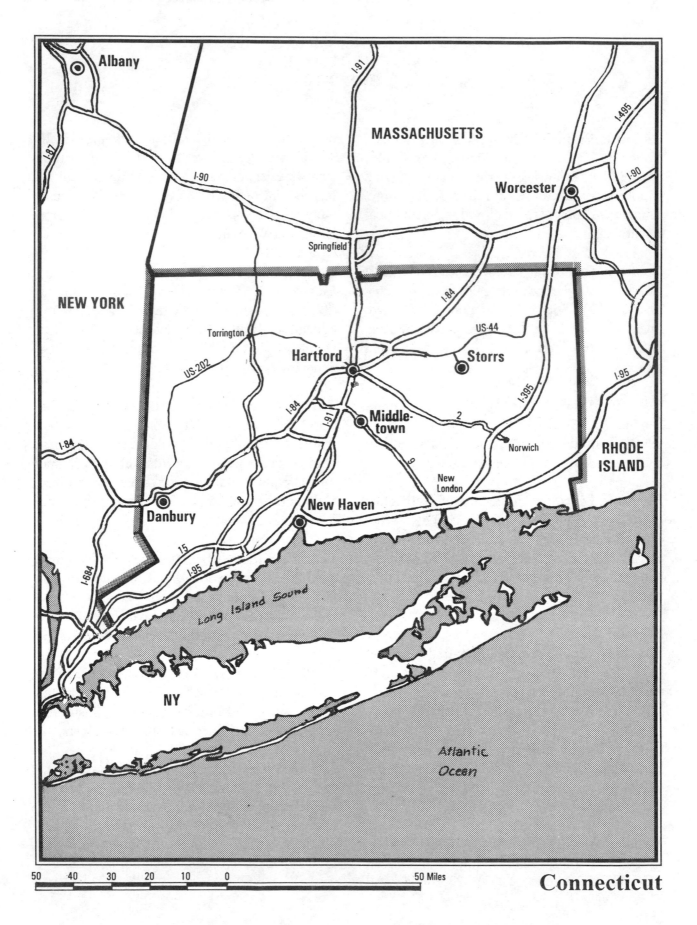

Connecticut

Connecticut

Connecticut State Historical Society, One Elizabeth St., Hartford, CT 06105. Phone: (860) 236-5621. Town records, biographies, manuscripts, families, early settlers, and churches.

American Antiquarian Society Library, 185 Salisbury St., Worcester, MA 01609-1634. Phone: (508) 755-5221. Many Connecticut records, including vital records, early newspapers, and town histories.

Connecticut State Library, 231 Capitol Ave., Hartford, CT 06106. Phone: (860) 566-4777. Great genealogy collection, with newspapers, books, manuscripts, town histories, maps, and many genealogies.

New Haven Colony Historical Society, Whitney Library, 114 Whitney Ave., New Haven, CT 06510-1025. Phone: (203) 562-4183. Of any records that exist for the earliest Southern Connecticut towns, this library has the best collection.

Godfrey Memorial Library, 134 Newfield St., Middletown, CT 06457. Phone: (860) 346-4375. Compilers of the *American Genealogical and Biographical Index.* This is an excellent genealogy library, with many references to New England records, plus guidebooks, indexes, biographies, genealogies, and much more.

Homer Babbidge Library, University of Connecticut, 369 Fairfield Rd., Storrs, CT 06298. Phone: (860) 486-2219. An outstanding genealogy collection relating to Connecticut.

Sterling Memorial Library, Yale University, 130 Wall St., PO Box 208240, New Haven, CT 06520. Phone: (203) 432-1775. Puritans and Congregational Church records, Connecticut,

New Haven, and New England history. Manuscripts, diaries, and journals.

General Services Center- Reference Research Section, Drawer 33, Montpelier, VT 05633-7601. Phone: (802) 828-2291. This is the Vermont State Historical Society and is a good research center for locating early Connecticut people.

Genealogy/History Library, Bennington Museum, W. Main St., Bennington, VT 05201. Phone: (802) 447-1571. An excellent place to find Connecticut families moving up the Connecticut river and to points west.

Albany Institute of History and Art, McKinney Library, 125 Washington Ave., Albany, NY 12210. Phone: (518) 463-4478. The facility has the best indexes to the original records from the early 1600s including references to Connecticut families moving into old Albany County during the colonial period (Albany County once included all of upper New York and all of Vermont).

Western Reserve Historical Society Library, 10825 East Blvd., Cleveland, OH 44106-1788. Phone: (216) 721-5722. The Western Reserve was a region of Ohio settled by refugees of the Revolutionary War from the state of Connecticut. Land records dating back to the 1790s for the Western Reserve area. The Collection excels in American Revolution, black and ethnic, Civil War, and slavery.

Western Connecticut State University Library, 181 White St., Danbury, CT 06810-6885. Phone: (203) 837-8200. Histories, biographies, genealogies, and local histories.

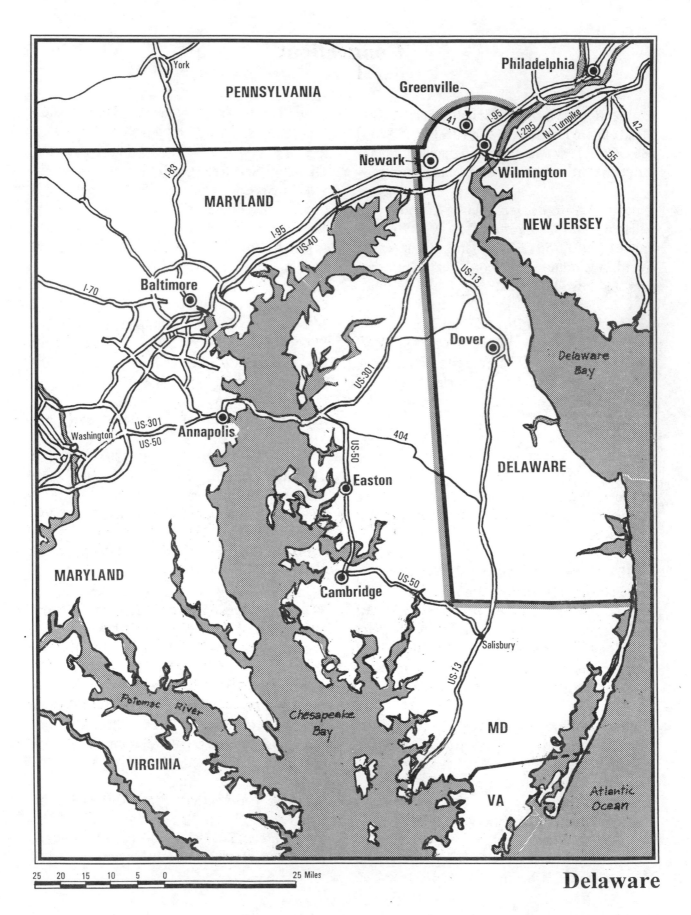

Delaware

Delaware

Historical Society of Pennsylvania Library, 1300 Locust St., Philadelphia, PA 19107-5699. Phone: (215) 732-6200. Original records of early Quakers, Germans, Scotch-Irish, and other colonial settlers in Penn's colonies. An excellent place to locate early settlers in Pennsylvania, New Jersey, and Delaware. More info here on early Delaware than in Delaware.

Historical Society of Delaware Library, 505 N. Market St., Wilmington, DE 19801. Phone: (302) 655-7161. This is an important resource for early Delaware. Collection includes colonial records, newspapers, church records, state records, Revolutionary War records, Civil War records, Delaware histories, and genealogies.

Pennsylvania State Archives, 3rd and Forster Sts., PO Box 1026, Harrisburg, PA 17108. Phone: (717) 783-3281. Colonial records include many references to Delaware settlements.

Delaware State Archives, Hall of Records, Dover, DE 19901. Phone: (302) 739-5318. Good coverage of colonial records for every hundred and every county.

Wilmington Institute Library, 10th and Market St., Wilmington, DE 19801. Phone: (302) 571-7400. Delawareana, genealogies, histories, and more.

Free Library of Philadelphia, Logan Square, Philadelphia, PA 19103-1157. Phone: (215) 686-5322. Historic Delaware references are numerous, with manuscripts, books, Quakers, early settlements, and more.

Maryland Historical Society, 201 W. Monument St., Baltimore, MD 21201. Phone: (410) 685-3750. Large genealogical collection for Delaware. Family Bibles, newspapers, biographies, genealogies, and more.

Hall of Records, Maryland State Archives, 350 Rowe Blvd., Annapolis, MD 21401. Phone: (410) 974-3914. This is a good resource center for locating early Delaware settlers.

Hagley Museum and Library, Greenville, Delaware. Mailing address: PO Box 3630, Wilmington, DE 19807-0630. Phone: (302) 658-2400. Early Delaware records, diaries, plat maps, and colonial records not in State Archives. Like another state archives for Delaware.

University of Delaware Library, College Ave., Newark, DE. 19717-5267. Phone: (302) 831-2965 (reference desk). Like another state archives.

Dover Public Library, 45 S. State St., Dover, DE 19901-3526. Phone: (302) 736-7030. Delaware and Delmarva Pennisula, Delawareana, local histories, and genealogies.

William C. Jason Library, Delaware State College, 1200 N. DuPont Highway, Dover, DE 19901. Phone: (302) 739-5112. Very good Delaware historical collection.

Talbot County Free Library, 100 W. Dover St., Easton, MD 21601-2620. Phone: (410) 822-1626. Many Delaware and Eastern Shore historical references.

Dorchester County Public Library, 303 Gay St., Cambridge, MD 21613. Phone: (410) 228-7331. Many Delaware and Eastern Shore historical references.

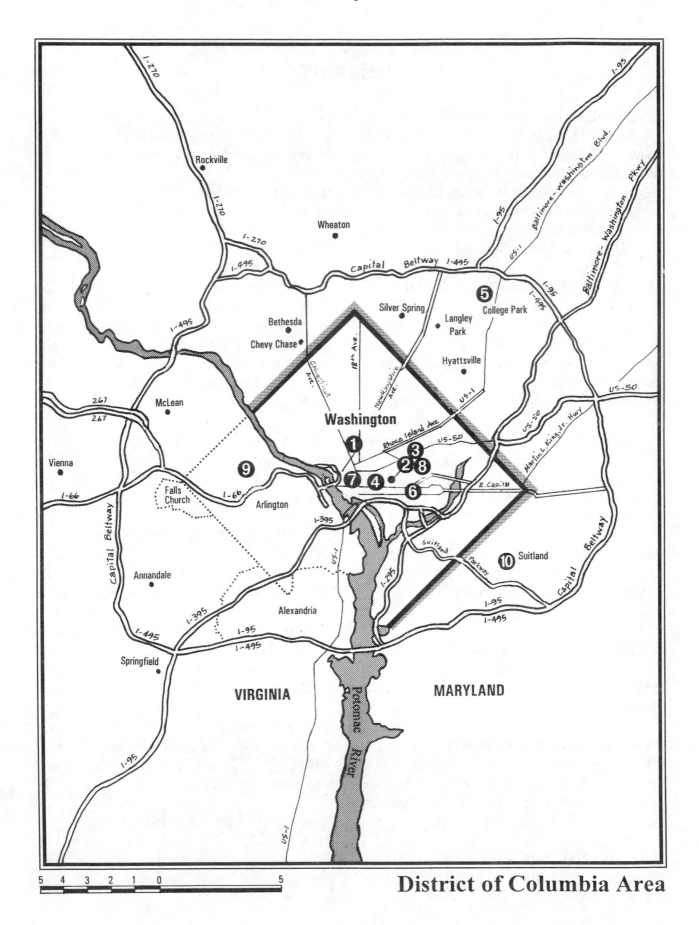

District of Columbia Area

District of Columbia Area

❶ **Historical Society of Washington, DC**, Library of Washington History, 1307 New Hampshire Ave., N.W., Washington, DC 20036. Phone: (202) 785-2068. This facility is like a state archives for the District of Columbia, containing many original documents that can be used for genealogical research, including vital records, biographies, histories, newspapers, and more.

❷ **Recorder of Deeds**, 6ᵗʰ and D Streets, Washington, DC 20004. Phone: (202) 727-5374. This is an important resource center for locating any resident of the District of Columbia who owned property, including the buyers from the first DC land auction sales.

❸ **Register of Wills**, 5ᵗʰ and E Streets, Washington, DC 20001. Phone: (202) 879-1499. Recorded wills of former residents of Washington, DC are located here.

❹ **Archives I Reference Branch,** National Archives and Records Administration, 8ᵗʰ St. and Pennsylvania Ave., N.W., Washington, DC 20408. Phone: (202) 501-5400. Over 65,000 rolls of microfilm with genealogical data. And:

❺ **Archives II Reference Branch**, 8601 Adelphi Road, College Park, MD 20740. Phone: (301) 713-7250 (textual reference). These two facilities represent the main branches of the National Archives.

❻ **Library of Congress**, Local History and Genealogy Room, Thomas Jefferson Building, 101 Independence Ave. S.E., Washington, D.C. 20540. Phone: (202) 707-6400. The Local History and Genealogy room is located on the ground floor. This facility is best for its guides and indexes, but the main Library of Congress electronic card catalogue is the key to locating book titles on any subject — the resources in this library are unmatched by any other library in the world.

❼ **National Society of the Daughters of the American Revolution**, Genealogical Research Library, 1776 D St., N.W., Washington, DC. Phone: (202) 879-3229. See America's Top Ten listings.

❽ **District of Columbia Public Library**, 901 G St., N.W., Washington, DC 20001. Phone: (202) 727-1213. Census films and indexes to vital records and wills, plus DC newspapers, 1800 to present. With all of the important DC facilities, this one is often forgotten. But it is a must stop for anyone with DC ancestors.

❾ **National Genealogical Society Library**, 4527 17ᵗʰ St. N., Arlington, VA 22207-2399. Phone: (703) 841-9065. Family histories, county histories, transcribed source materials, and reference volumes. This is an excellent library for genealogical research. Non-members may visit.

❿ **Washington National Records Center**, 4205 Suitland Rd., Suitland, MD 20746-8001. Phone: (301) 457-7000. This facility has the criminal and civil court records from the district court of Washington, DC, providing an excellent source for locating early DC people.

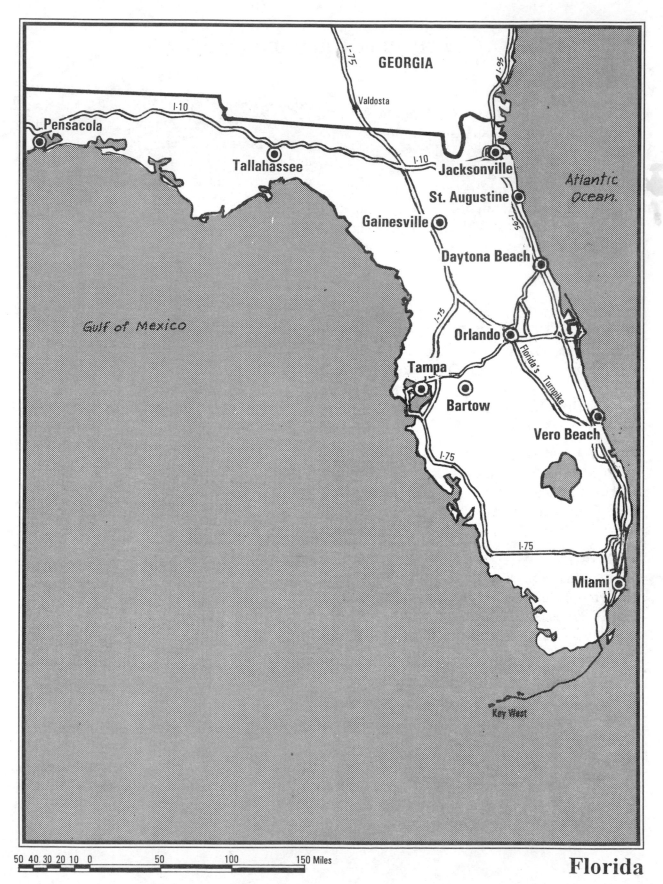

Florida

Florida

Florida State Archives, 500 S. Bronough St., R.A. Gray Building, Tallahassee, FL 32399-0250. Phone: (904) 487-2073. An outstanding Florida genealogical collection with many original county and state documents . The place to start for locating Florida people.

Orlando Public Library, Orange County Library System, 101 E. Central Blvd., Orlando, FL 32801. Phone: (407) 425-4694. Largest overall genealogy reference library in the state. Good coverage of American genealogical sources. Censuses, biographies, histories, genealogies, and much more.

Indian River County Library, 1600 21st St., Vero Beach, FL 32960-3461. Phone: (561) 770-5060. A very large genealogy collection. Rivals Orlando in size and quality.

Jacksonville Public Library, 122 N. Ocean St., Jacksonville, FL 32202-3374. Phone: (904) 630-2409. Good coverage for Southeastern U.S., with many histories, biographies, genealogies, federal censuses and soundex films, plus, the oldest Floridiana collection in the state.

Hillsborough County Historical Commission Museum Library, County Courthouse, Tampa, FL 33602. Phone: (813) 272-3843. The best indexes to Florida people in the state.

Pace Library, University of West Florida, 1100 University Parkway, Pensacola, FL 32514-5750. Phone: (904) 474-2492. An excellent genealogy research facility. This is a starting place for locating references to the earliest Florida people (The Florida panhandle settlers).

St. Augustine Historical Society, Research Library, 271 Charlotte St., St. Augustine, FL 32084-5099. Phone: (904) 824-2872. An excellent collection of materials relating to the first east coast Florida colonists. Spanish records, including parish records of births, marriages, and deaths date back to 1594.

Yonge Library of Florida History, Smathers Library, University of Florida Library, 205 Library East, Gainesville, FL 32611. Phone: (352) 392-0319. Spanish colonial records, US borderlands, best Florida newspaper archives.

Polk County Historical and Genealogical Library, Old Courthouse, 100 E. Main St., Bartow, FL 33830. Phone: (914) 534-4380. Very good genealogy collection.

Pensacola Public Library, 200 W. Gregory, Pensacola, FL 32501-4878. Phone: (904) 435-1760. A good genealogy collection.

Volusia County Public Library, City Island, Daytona Beach, FL 32118. Phone: (904) 252-8374. The genealogy collection is very good, not just Florida, but for the entire eastern seaboard.

Miami Dade Public Library, 101 W. Flagler St., Miami, FL 33130. Phone: (305) 375-5580. All U.S. Censuses on microfilm plus an excellent Florida collection.

Special Collections, University of South Florida Library, 4202 E. Fowler Ave., Tampa, FL 33620-5400. Phone: (813) 974-2731. Strong collection of published Florida local histories and Hillsborough County records, 1840-1980.

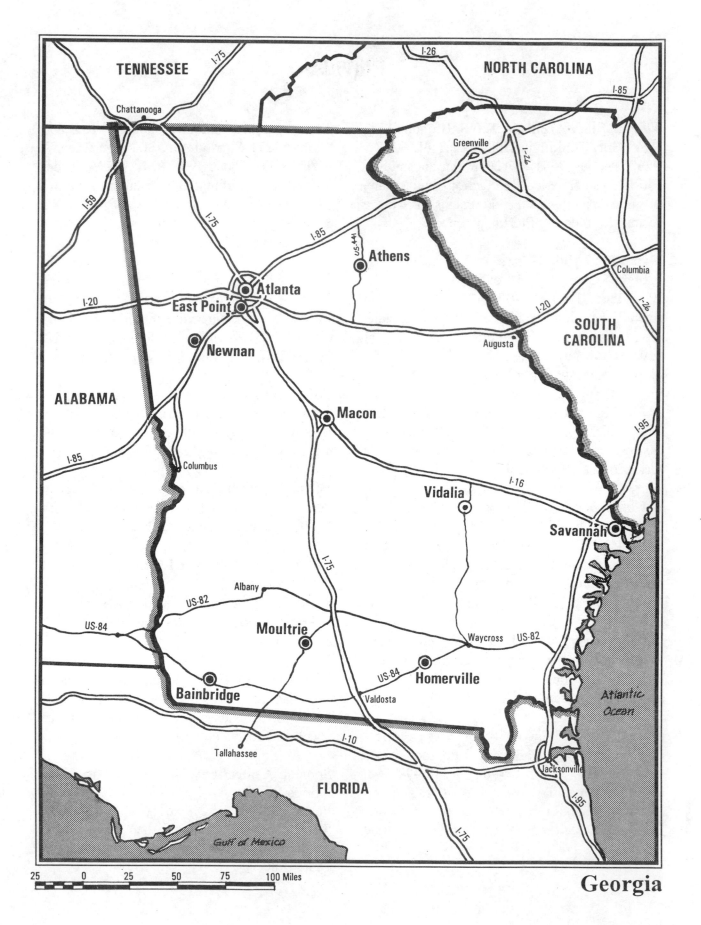

Georgia

Georgia

Georgia Department of Archives and History, Public Services Division Library, 330 Capitol Ave., S.E., Atlanta, GA 30334. Phone: (404) 656-2393. State government records, county records, newspapers, Georgia histories, family histories, county histories, and more. This is the place with the records to start locating early Georgia people.

Georgia Historical Society Library, 501 Whitaker St., Savannah, GA 31499. Phone: (912) 651-2128. Nearly as many genealogical resources as the Atlanta archives.

Atlanta-Fulton Public Library, 1 Margaret Mitchell Square, N.W., Atlanta, GA 30303-1089. Phone: (404) 730-1700. Historic Georgia and Genealogy Collections are large. Good coverage for the Southeastern part of the U.S.

Coweta County Genealogical Research Center, Clark Street, Maggie Brown Building, PO Box 1014, Newnan, GA 30264. Best set of Family Group Sheets for all of Georgia.

Main Library, University of Georgia, Jackson St., Athens, GA 30602. Phone: (706) 542-2716. For references to early Georgia settlers, this is the largest manuscript collection in the state, plus county histories, county records, family records, biographies, newspapers, and more.

Washington Memorial Library, Middle Georgia Regional Library System, 1180 Washington Ave., Macon, GA 31201-1794. Phone: (912) 714-0800. One of the best library collections in the state for genealogy, African-American, and local history.

National Archives, Southeast Region, 1557 St. Joseph Ave., East Point, GA 30344. Hours: Mon. - Fri., 8:00am - 4:00pm, and Tuesdays, 8:00am - 8:00pm. All microfilms of U.S. federal censuses, 1790-1920, and all printed and soundex indexes.

Ellen Payne Odom Genealogy Library, PO Box 1110, Moultrie, GA 31776. Phone: (912) 985-6540. This library publishes *The Family Tree*, a free tabloid newspaper for Scottish clans and genealogy subjects — the genealogical periodical with the largest circulation in America (over 70,000 and growing daily). The library is the repository for several Scottish clans, and its collection is one of the best in America for Scottish references. A good basic America genealogy collection is located here as well.

Huxford Genealogical Society Library, PO Box 595, Homerville, GA 31634. Phone: (912) 487-2310. Genealogical references for the southeast of the U.S. are well covered.

John E. Ladson, Jr. Genealogical and Historical Foundation Library, 610 Jackson St., Vidalia, GA 30474. (Branch of Ohoopee Regional Library. Phone: (912) 537-9283. Mostly books, but the collection covers nearly the entire Atlantic seaboard for anything related to genealogy.

Southwest Georgia Regional Library, 301 S/. Monroe St., Bainbridge, GA 31717. Phone: (912) 248-2665. A very good collection of books, surname folders, genealogies, newspapers, oral histories, and more.

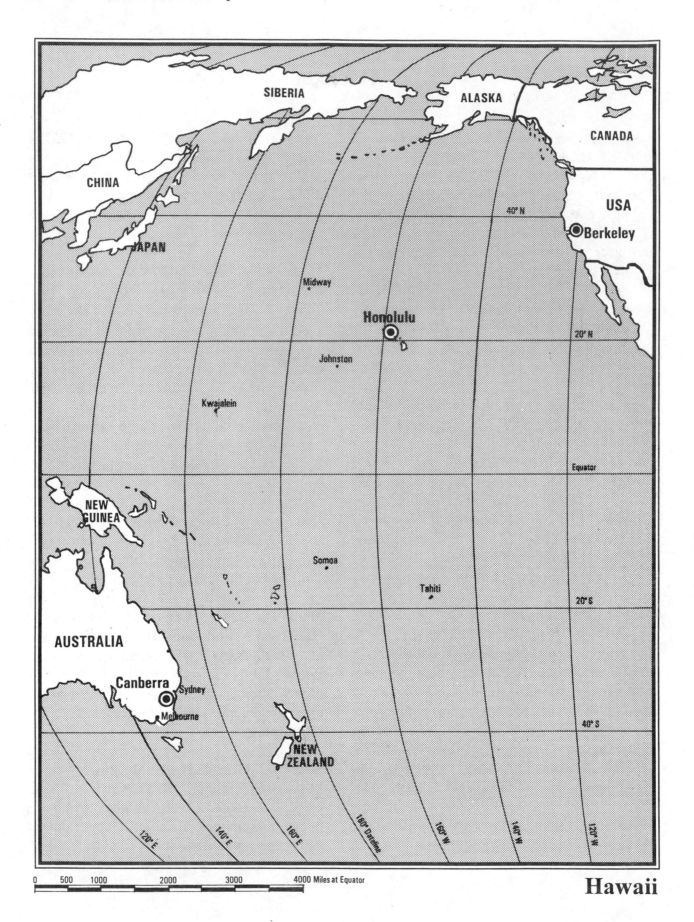

SIBERIA

ALASKA

CANADA

CHINA

USA

40° N

⊚Berkeley

JAPAN

Midway

Honolulu

20° N

Johnston

Kwajalein

Equator

NEW
GUINEA

Somoa

Tahiti

20° S

AUSTRALIA

Canberra

Sydney

⊚

Melbourne

40° S

NEW
ZEALAND

120° E   140° E   160° E   180° Dateline   160° W   140° W   120° W

0   500   1000   2000   3000   4000 Miles at Equator

Hawaii

Hawaii

Bancroft Library, University of California, Berkeley, CA 94720. Phone: (415) 642-3781. The "Bancroft Collection" is outstanding for early settlers. This is the premier library for records of the West, including shipping and other records relating to people going to the Sandwich Islands from about 1850 forward.

Hawaii State Archives, Iolani Palace Grounds, Honolulu, HI 96813. Phone: (808) 586-0329. A good genealogy collection. Immigration records from 1900, newspapers, Hawaii government collection, and Captain James Cook collection.

Hawaii State Library, 478 S. King St., Honolulu, HI 96813. Phone: (808) 586-3500. Mostly secondary sources, but the largest genealogy collection in Hawaii. Newspapers, maps, and book collection is outstanding.

Hamilton Library, University of Hawaii, 2550 The Mall, Honolulu, HI 96822. Phone: (808) 956-8111. Filled with manuscripts on Hawaiians, Japanese, Chinese, and early Americans in Hawaii. Good place to find immigrants to Hawaii.

Bishop Museum Library, 1525 Bernice St., Honolulu, HI 96817-2704. Phone: (808) 848-4147. Primary source collection documenting cultural and natural history in the Pacific. Collection of manuscripts and Museum records include: personal 19th-century materials from Hawaiian royal family collections; museum-generated records of scientific research, plantation, and corporate records of major sugar companies in Hawaii; genealogies; Hawaiian-language materials; published and manuscript maps of the Pacific; audio collection of both commercial and field recordings; a million photographic images; 900 titles of motion picture films; about 250 oils on canvas, and 4,000 works of art on paper.

Pacific Manuscripts Bureau, Coombs Building, Research School of Pacific and Asian Studies, The Australian National University, Canberra, ACT 0200, Australia. Phone: International code 61, area code 612, local 6249-2521. A large collection of genealogies and many other manuscripts written by Pacific Islanders (including Hawaiians) in their own language.

Hawaiian Historical Society Library, 560 Kawaiahao St., Honolulu, HI 96813. Phone: (808) 537-6271. History of Hawaii and Pacific Collection for late 18th and 19th century. Biographical indexes to early Hawaiians, plus obituaries, newspapers, and more. Many documents of Portugese, Chinese, Japanese, and Polynesian. Strong on pre-American era.

Daughters of Hawaii, 2913 Pali Highway, Honolulu, Hawaii 96817. Phone: (808) 595-6291. Records on Hulihee Palace Museum in Kailua-Kona, the Queen Emma Summer Palace in Honolulu, and the Daughters of Hawaii. Genealogies and lineages of members on file. Institution and collection founded in 1903. Open by appointment only.

Hawaiian Mission Children's Society Library, 553 S. King Street, Honolulu, HI 96813. Phone: (808) 531-0481. Records, personal journals, letters, and photos of early 19th-century Congregational missionaries to the Hawaiian Islands including books, pamphlets, photos; newspapers; and microfilm.

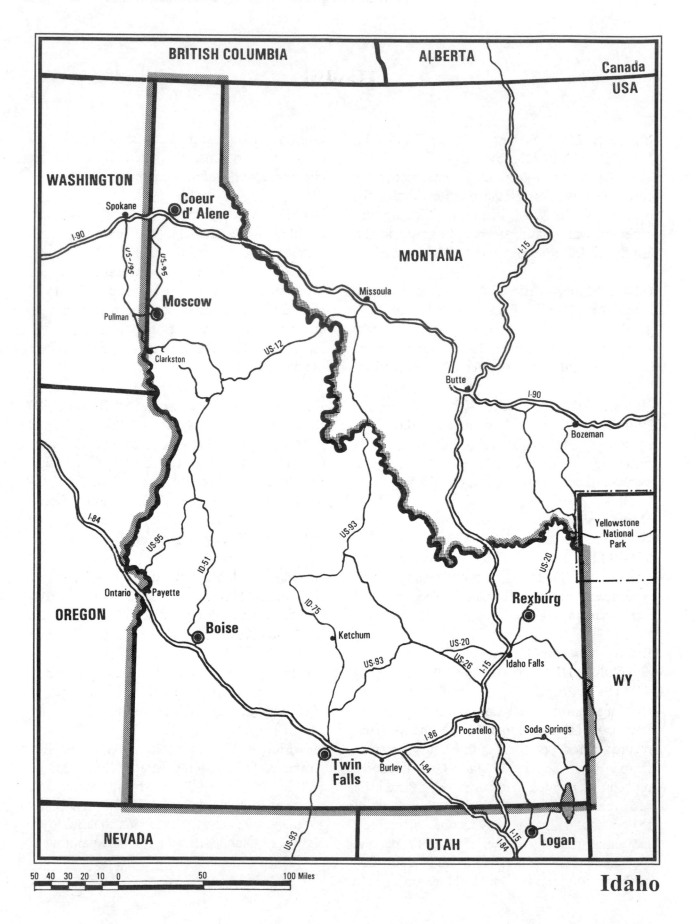

Idaho

Idaho

Idaho State Historical Society and **Idaho State Library**, Library and Archives Building, 450 N. 4th St., Boise, ID 83702-7695. Phone: (208) 334-3356. A variety of materials of value to anyone investigating personal, family, community, state, or regional history. All extant Idaho newspapers, dating back to the earliest days of Idaho Territory, are available on microfilm; thousands of photographs from across the state can be examined and copies ordered; and a large collection of maps illustrates Idaho's growth. Genealogical resources include family and local histories, various census records from 1790 to 1920, parish registers, cemetery records, and many other helpful sources of information: county records, genealogies, biographies, family folders, and the Idaho Death Index, 1911-1932.

University of Idaho Library, Rayburn St., Moscow, ID 83844-2350. Phone: (208) 885-6534. Mountain men, early settlers. The special collections include Idaho-Northwest histories, rare books, and many documents relating to Idaho.

McKay Library, Ricks College, Rexburg, ID 83460-0405. Phone: (208) 356-2351. Heavy on pioneer settlements, farmers, ranchers, Mormons, and oral histories.

Cache Valley Library, (Family History Center), 50 North Main, Logan, UT 84322. Phone: (435) 750-9870. This library has a unique collection relating to early Utah, Idaho, and Wyoming. Ranching, early settlers, cattlemen, farmers, trails, and railroading.

Bancroft Library, University of California, Berkeley, CA 94720. Phone: (415) 642-3781. The "Bancroft Collection" is outstanding for early settlers. This is the premier library for records of the West, including many records relating to Idaho.

National Archives, Pacific Alaska Region (Seattle), 6125 Sand Point Way, N.E., Seattle, WA 98115. Phone: (206) 526-6501. All microfilm for U.S. federal censuses, 1790-1920 plus all soundex indexes and virtually all printed statewide census indexes. The archives also has many historical records of the federal courts of Idaho.

Oregon Historical Society Library, 1200 S.W. Park Ave., Portland, OR 97205. Phone: (503) 222-1741. Manuscripts, family folders, histories, and biographies. Many original diaries and journals from Oregon Trail families., and guides to overland documents of pioneers through Idaho.

Suzzallo Library, University of Washington, Seattle, WA 98195-0001. Phone: (206) 543-1760. The Pacific Northwest and Alaska coverage for historical materials is outstanding. Many Idaho references can be found here, particularly for the early lumbering industry of Idaho, miners, setters, and Idaho history.

North Idaho College Library, 1000 West Garden Ave., Coeur d'Alene, ID 83814. Phone: (208) 769-3355. Taped oral histories, newspapers, Idaho histories, biographies, county histories. Not well known by genealogists in the area, but one of the best overall genealogy collections in the state.

Twin Falls Public Library, 434 2nd St E., Twin Falls, ID 83301. Phone: (208) 733-2965. Early Idaho historical collection, newspapers, books, and manuscripts for early Northwest people.

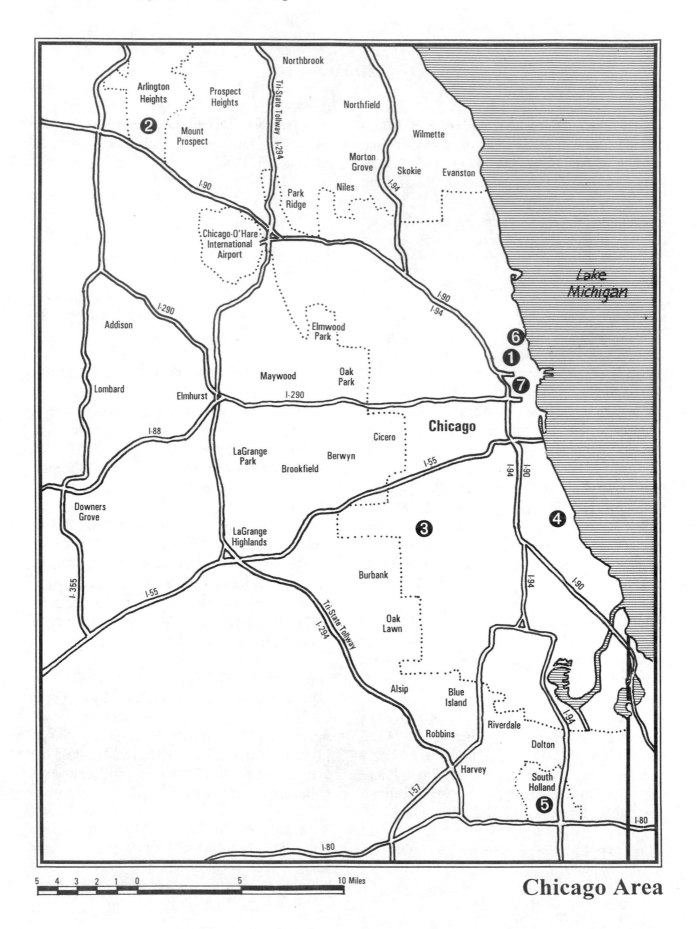

Chicago Area

Illinois (Chicago Area)

Note: Numbers indicate the location of each facility on the map

❶ **The Newberry Library**, 68 W. Walton St., Chicago, IL 60610-3394. Phone: (312) 255-3512. The Newberry Library has over 17,000 printed family genealogies. The collection is especially noteworthy for its coverage of colonial America, particularly New England. The local history collection includes county, city, town, church, and other local histories from all regions of the United States, as well as from Canada and the British Isles. The Newberry holds a comprehensive collection of New England town histories, as well as an especially strong collection of county histories from the Midwest and Mid-Atlantic states. Newberry's collection of Civil War unit histories is one of the country's best.

❷ **Arlington Heights Memorial Library**, 500 N. Dunton Ave., Arlington Heights, IL 60004-5966. Phone: (847) 392-0100. Local history and genealogy collection is huge. Printed genealogies, manuscripts, periodicals, newspapers, special aids, surname folders, and a great overall genealogy collection.

❸ **National Archives**, Great Lakes Region, 7358 South Pulaski Road, Chicago, Illinois 60629-5898. Phone: (773) 581-7816. All microfilm for U.S. federal censuses, 1790-1920, plus all soundex indexes and virtually all printed statewide census indexes.

❹ **University of Chicago Library**, 1100 E. 57th St., Chicago, IL 60637-1502. Phone: (773) 702-4085. The historical records in this library are numerous. Of special interest to genealogists is *The Durrett Collection* which contains historical manuscripts relating to Kentucky and the Ohio River Valley. The size and content of this collection is comparable to the Draper Collection in the State Historical Society of Wisconsin, yet it is not as well known by genealogists. The collection includes many references to the earliest people of the Ohio Valley.

❺ **South Suburban Genealogical and Historical Society Library**, Roosevelt Community Center, 320 E. 161st Place, PO Box 96, South Holland, IL 60473. Phone: (708) 333-9474. This library has a very good collection for genealogists, including local histories, genealogies, naturalization records, Pullman Car Works personnel records, obituary files, church histories, and more.

❻ **Chicago Historical Society**, Archives and Manuscripts, Clark St. at North Ave., Chicago, IL 60614-6099. Phone: (312) 642-4600. The archives holds more than twenty million manuscripts, including letters, account books, autograph books, certificates, diaries, genealogical charts, invitations, journals, licenses, and other printed forms filled-in with individual information, log books, membership lists, memoirs, memoranda, minutes, muster rolls, research notes, scrapbooks, scripts, sermons, speeches, subscription lists, and telegrams. The collection is particularly informative on U.S. history through the Civil War era, especially the Chicago area's early history, and Chicago-area social conditions.

❼ **Chicago Title and Trust**, 171 N. Clark St., Chicago, IL 60601. Phone: (800) 621-1919. Property records prior to the Chicago Fire of 1871. They will research early records for a fee.

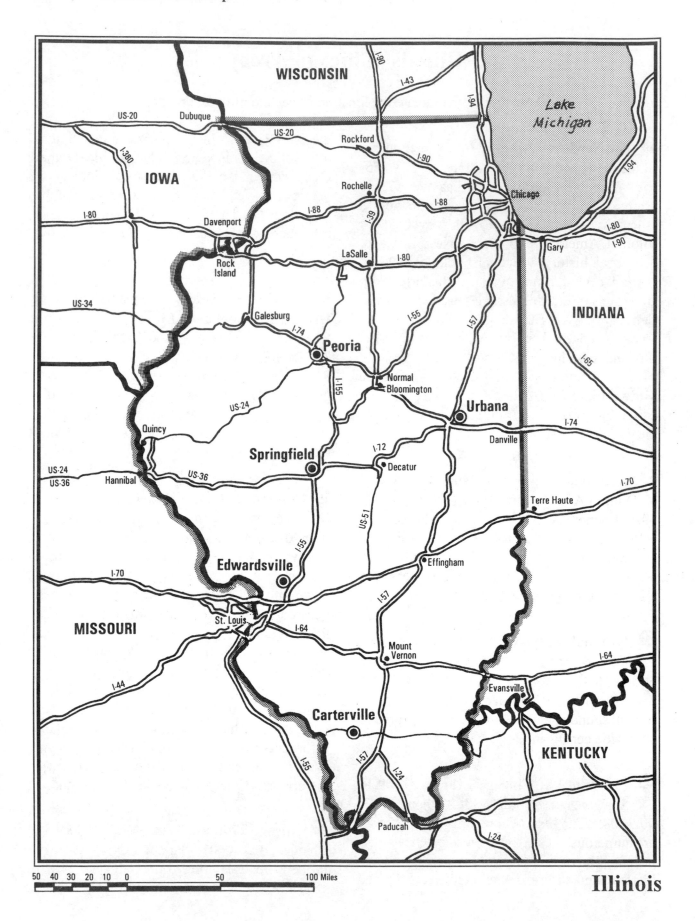

Illinois

Illinois (except Chicago)

Illinois State Archives, Norton Building, Springfield, IL 62756. Phone: (217) 782-4682. County and state records. Pre-Chicago fire records. Indexed vital records. The earliest land grants are recorded here. Muster rolls and military records in the collection include a large number of Civil War registers. All Illinois federal and state censuses are available. A surname card index exists for much of the collection.

Illinois State Library, 300 S. 2nd St., Springfield, IL 62701. Phone: (217) 782-7596. The State Library collects the official publications of state and federal government. It holds microform copies of many State Archives records. Collections include census film for Illinois through 1920, 19th and 20th century Illinois county plat books, Illinois county histories, Sanborn Fire Insurance atlases, and Revolutionary War Pension and Bounty Warrants microfilm.

Illinois State Historical Library, Old State Capitol, Springfield, IL 62701. Phone: (217) 782-4836. Excellent reference library for locating Illinois people. The Historical Library contains many published sources. These sources include an extensive collection of county histories, with an every-name index. The Illinois Daughters of the American Revolution and the State Genealogical Society donate their publications to the Historical Library. The Library has the largest microfilm collection of Illinois newspapers in the state, some dating prior to statehood. Many family papers are contained in the large manuscript collection.

University Library, University of Illinois, Urbana-Champaign, 1408 W. Gregory Dr., Urbana, IL 61801. Phone: (217) 333-0790. One of the top book collections in America, including county histories, farmers' registers, and more. It is like another archives for Illinois.

Lincoln Library, 326 S. 7th St., Springfield, IL 62701. Phone: (217) 753-4910. The Sangamon Valley Collection provides in depth resources for the study of Sangamon and the surrounding counties. Obituaries in the Illinois State Journal are indexed for the years 1861-1934 and 1959 to the present. All Springfield City Directories are available.

Lovejoy Library, Southern Illinois University at Edwardsville, Edwardsville, IL 62026-1063. Phone: (618) 692-2603 (information). Top library for Southern Illinois: large genealogical collection, with newspapers, biographies, county histories, family folders, maps, and more.

Peoria Public Library, 107 N.E. Monroe St., Peoria, IL 61602-1070. Phone: (309) 672-8835. Large genealogy and local history department, with many indexes, DAR files, and basic genealogy for the plains states.

The Urbana Free Library, 201 S. Race St., Urbana, IL 61801-3283. Phone: (217) 367-4057. Genealogy and Champaign County history, with genealogical sources for the entire U.S. A very good basic genealogy resource center, with printed genealogies, manuscripts, family folders, and microfilms.

Logan College Library, 700 Logan College Rd., Carterville, IL 62918. Phone: (618) 985-2828. A focal point for genealogy in southern Illinois. The genealogy collection is huge.

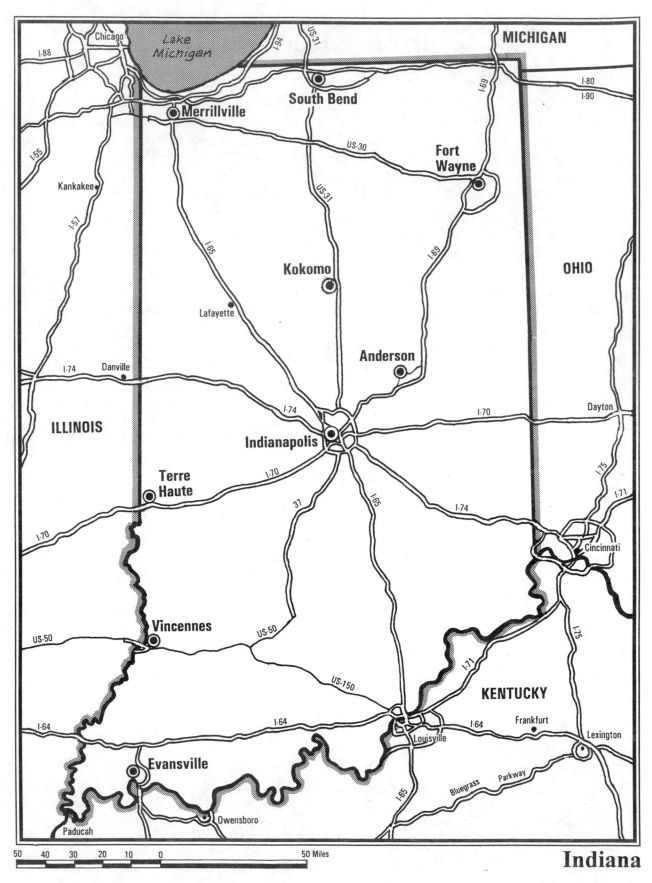

Chicago

Lake Michigan

MICHIGAN

I-88

Chicago

I-94

US-31

I-69

I-80

I-90

South Bend

Merrillville

US-30

Fort Wayne

I-55

I-57

Kankakee

US-31

I-65

I-69

OHIO

Kokomo

Lafayette

Anderson

Danville

I-74

I-74

Dayton

ILLINOIS

I-70

Indianapolis

I-70

I-75

Terre Haute

I-70

37

I-65

I-74

I-71

I-70

Cincinnati

Vincennes

US-50

US-50

US-150

I-71

KENTUCKY

I-64

I-64

I-64

Frankfort

Louisville

Lexington

Evansville

I-65

Bluegrass Parkway

Owensboro

Paducah

50 40 30 20 10 0   50 Miles

Indiana

Indiana

Indiana State Library and Historical Building. This building houses three separate agencies, each having excellent genealogical resources:

- **Indiana Historical Society Library**, 315 W. Ohio St., Indianapolis, IN 46202-3299. Phone: (317) 232-1879. Many original materials.

- **Indiana State Archives**, 140 N. Senate Ave., Indianapolis, IN 46204. Phone: (317) 232-3660. Houses military records, federal land records, and original records from counties.

- **Indiana State Library**, 140 N. Senate Ave., Indianapolis, IN 46204-2296. Its Indiana Division has three sections housing excellent Indiana genealogy resources: (1) *Genealogy Section.* Phone: (317) 232-3689. Great collection, great indexes. (2) *Indiana Section.* Phone: (317) 232-3671. Extensive collection of Indiana manuscripts and published histories. (3) *Newspapers Section*. Phone: (317) 232-3664. Most extensive collection of Indiana newspapers in original and microfilm formats.

Allen County Public Library, 900 Webster St., Fort Wayne, IN 46802. Phone: (219) 424-7241, ext. 2242. (See America's Top Ten).

Lewis Historical Collections Library, Vincennes University, LRC-22, Vincennes, IN 47591-9986. Phone: (812) 888-4330. Family folders, cemeteries, early Indiana, printed genealogies, many not in Indianapolis.

Frederick Elbel Library, Northern Indiana Historical Society, 808 W. Washington St., South Bend, IN 46601. Phone: (219) 235-9664. Very large military collection, newspapers, special indexes, plus a large collection of books, periodicals, maps, and more.

Willard Library, 21 1st Ave., Evansville, IN 47710. Phone: (812) 425-4309. A specialized research library, primarily for genealogy. Filled with biographies, genealogies, and county histories.

Lake County Public Library, 1919 W. 81st Ave., Merrillville, IN 46410-5382. Phone: (219) 769-3541. Large collection of books, microfilms, and surname folders.

St. Joseph County Public Library, 304 S. Main St., South Bend, IN 46601. Phone: (219) 282-4646. Comparable to Ft. Wayne library for statewide Indiana records.

Vigo County Public Library, 1 Library Square, Terre Haute, IN 47807. Phone: (812) 232-1113, ext. 212. Its Special Collections Department houses extensive published sources for Vigo and surrounding counties in Indiana and Illinois as well as city directories and newspapers.

Anderson Public Library, 111 E. 12th St., Anderson, IN 46016-2701. Phone: (765) 641-2442. Its Indiana Room houses extensive published genealogies and county histories from Indiana. It houses the extensive library of Willard Heiss.

Kokomo Howard County Public Library, 220 N. Union St., Kokomo, IN 46901-4614. Phone: (765) 454-4710 (Reference). A strong collection for genealogical research, this library has increased in size dramatically in the past few years. Censuses, biographies, histories, and many published Indiana sources can be found here.

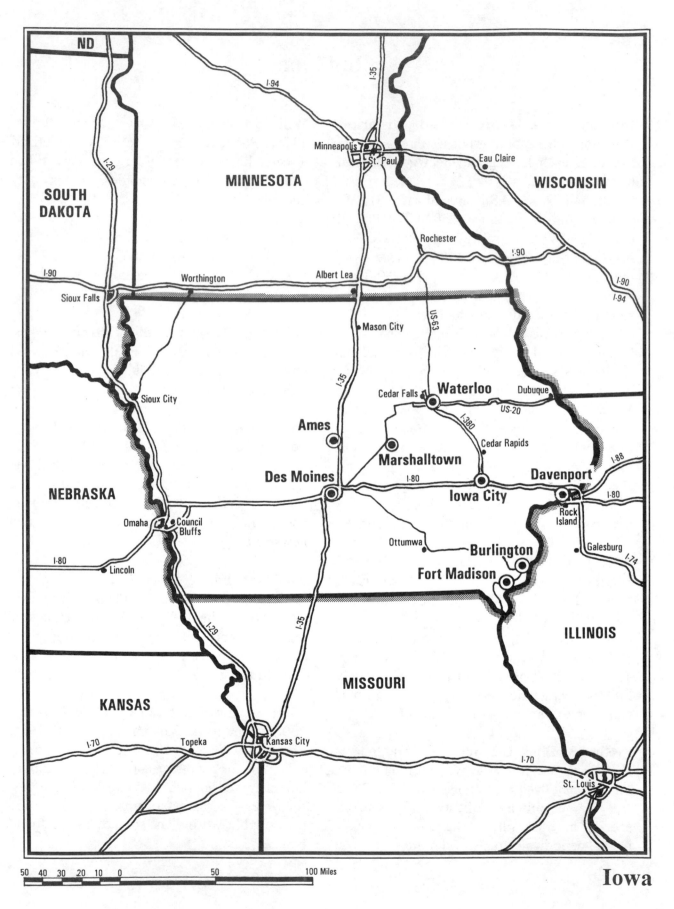

Iowa

Iowa

State Historical Society of Iowa - Des Moines, Library Archives Bureau, Capitol Complex, 600 E. Locust, Des Moines, IA 50319. Phone: (515) 281-5111. The largest collection of microfilm of county records, plus books, periodicals, and manuscripts. This is the starting point for genealogical research in Iowa.

State Historical Society of Iowa - Iowa City, Library Archives Bureau, 402 Iowa Ave., Iowa City, IA 52240-5391. Phone: (319) 335-3916. Not a repeat of Des Moines. Manuscripts, newspapers, government, business, biographies, and genealogies. This is an outstanding collection of Iowa materials for genealogists.

Iowa Genealogical Society Library, 6000 Douglas Ave., Suite 145, PO Box 7735, Des Moines, IA 50322. Phone: (515) 276-0287. Genealogies, periodicals, histories, county indexes, and many unpublished family histories not found anywhere else. This society is one of the largest in America and has published many indexes, extracts, and verbatim county records from all over Iowa. The library features many records for the states that contributed to the peopling of Iowa, including Illinois, Indiana, Ohio, New York, and the New England States.

Grout Museum of History and Science Library, 503 South St., Waterloo, IA 50701. Phone: (319) 234-6357. This facility is a sleeper, with wonderful records for genealogists. A huge resource library for more than just the Iowa area. A very large family surname folder collection plus many guides and indexes to cemeteries, county histories, and more.

Marshalltown Public Library, 36 N. Center St., Marshalltown, IA 50158. Phone: (515) 754-5738. Genealogy, DAR collection. A very good regional library with printed genealogies, periodicals, and family folders. Coverage for much more than Iowa.

Iowa State University Library, Ames, IA 50011-2140. Phone: (515) 294-1442 (general information). Huge book library with many county histories. Great newspaper collection for Iowa, and a great map library.

University of Iowa Library, 100 Main Library, Iowa City, IA 52242-1420. Phone: (319) 335-5867. Rare books, manuscripts, histories, and oral histories. Very large book and periodical collection. One of the largest German language book collections in America. Very good collection of newspapers, and the ethnic resources are strong.

Fort Madison Public Library, 614 7th St., Fort Madison, IA 52627. Phone: (319) 372-5721. A little country library, but for genealogy a regional library with many resources: books, manuscripts, surname folders, pedigree charts, special name indexes, and periodicals.

Burlington Public Library, 501 N. 4th St., Burlington, IA 52601. Phone: (319) 753-1647. A very good regional library for genealogical resources. References related to migrations, Germans, Dutch, French, and more. Located on the Mississippi River, this library has many references to river boats and river traffic.

Richardson-Sloane Genealogical Library, 1019 Mound St., Suite 301, Davenport, IA 52803-3923. Phone: (800) 828-4363. This library hopes to be the largest genealogical resource center between Ft. Wayne, Indiana and Independence, Missouri. They are off to a good start with a solid genealogy collection.

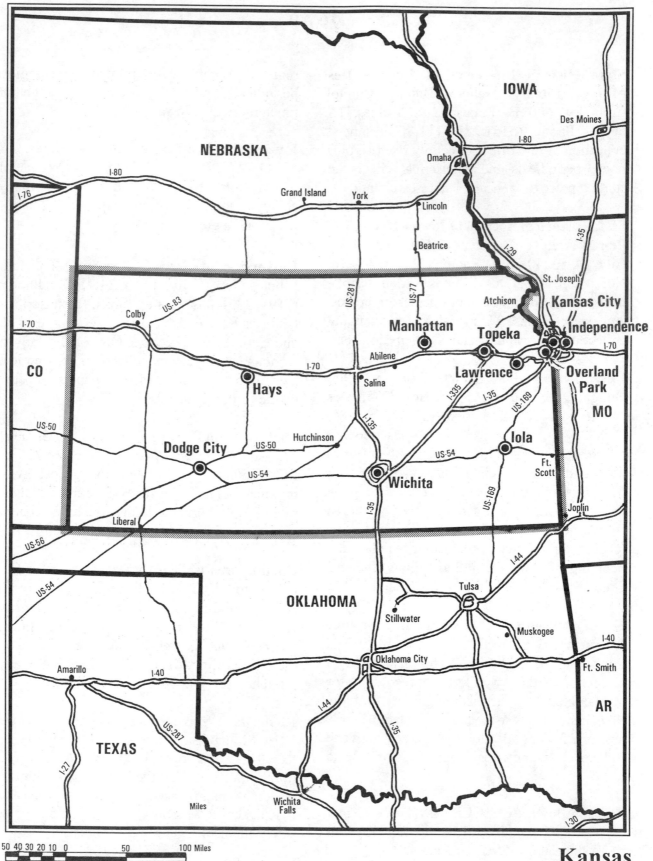

Kansas

Kansas

Kansas State Historical Society Library, 6425 S.W. 6th Ave., PO Box 3585, Topeka, KS 66615-1099. Phone: (785) 272-8681. Newspapers, county records, biographies, genealogies, land records, railroads, and more. This is the place to· start locating Kansas ancestors. Clearly the best facility in Kansas.

Kansas State Library, 300 S.W. 10th Ave., Room 343 North, State Capitol Building, Topeka, KS 66612. Phone: (913) 296-3296. Largest book library in the state, including county histories, ethnic resources, published guides and inventories, family genealogies, and more.

Kansas Genealogical Society Library, Village Square Mall - Lower Level, 2601 Central, PO Box 103, Dodge City, Kansas 67801. Phone: (316) 225-1951. Best collection of family folders and genealogical periodicals in Kansas.

Kansas Collection, Spencer Research Library, University of Kansas, Lawrence, KS 66045-2800. Phone: (913) 864-4274. Primary records, newspapers, manuscripts, histories, railroads, Native Americans, and pioneers.

Riley County Genealogical Society Library, 2005 Claffin Rd., Manhattan, KS 66502. Phone: (785) 565-6495. Pre-Civil War records for Kansas are excellent. Earliest settlers in Kansas well documented in obituaries, family folders, indexes, and more.

Wichita Public Library, 223 Main St., Wichita, KS 67202. Phone: (316) 262-061. Kansas and Local History collection has many Kansas genealogies. Mostly books and periodicals, special publications for southeast Kansas, Missouri, Arkansas, and Oklahoma.

Johnson County Library, Central Research Library, 9875 W. 97th St., Overland Park, KS 66212. Phone: (913) 495-2400. Kansas and genealogy collections. Mostly books and periodicals, with good coverage for Missouri, Tennessee, and Kentucky. Many microfilms, family folders, and more.

Kansas Heritage Center Library, 1000 2nd Ave., PO Box 1275, Dodge City, KS 67801. Phone: (316) 227-1616. Kansas cowboys, oral histories, Fort Dodge history, the old west, and more.

Forsyth Library, Fort Hays State University, 600 Park St., Hays, KS 67601-4099. Phone: (913) 628-4431. Western Collection, Western Kansas History, oral histories. Great genealogical collection, mostly from local genealogical and historical societies. Many denominational sources, Hutterite, Mennonite, Catholic, Lutheran, and more.

Iola Public Library, 218 E. Madison, Iola, KS 66749. Phone: (316) 365-5136. Good genealogy book collection for all of Kansas. Family folders, special indexes, and published records of many Kansas counties.

Missouri Valley Room, Kansas City Public Library, 311 E. 12th, Kansas City, MO 64106-2454. Phone: (816) 221-2685. Good genealogy collection with many Kansas references.

Mid-Continent Public Library, North Independence Branch, 15616 E. Highway 24, Independence, MO 64050. Phone: (816) 252-0950. (See listing under Missouri).

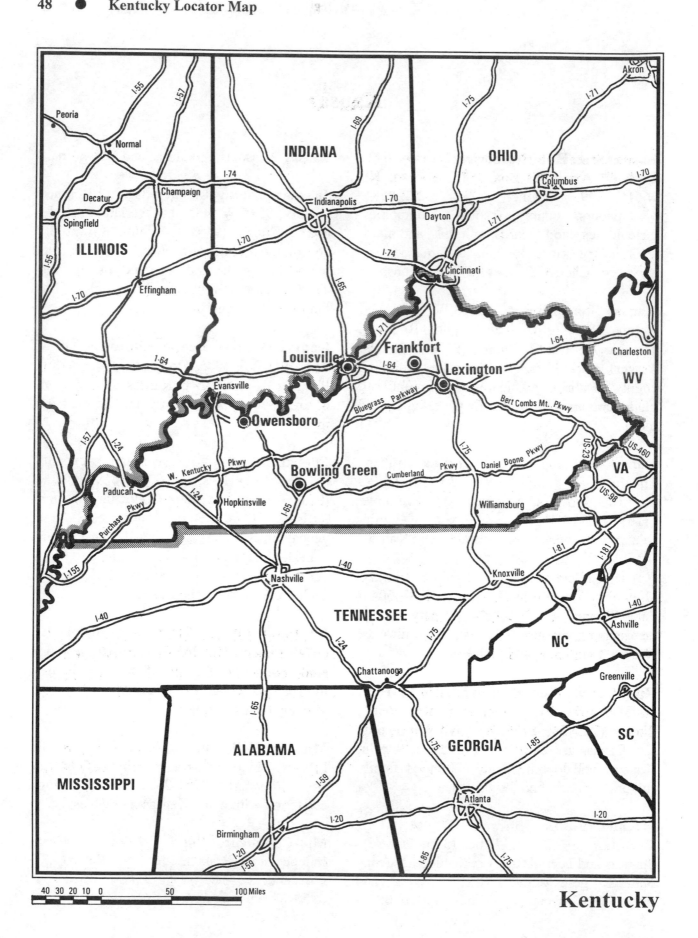

Kentucky

Kentucky

Kentucky Historical Society Library, Old Statehouse, 300 W. Broadway, PO Box 1792, Frankfort, KY 40602. Phone: (502) 564-3016. Largest collection of family folders in Kentucky. Every known printed Kentucky history and genealogy. Many newspapers, maps, city directories, and more. Kentucky's best!

Kentucky Department of Libraries and Archives, 300 Coffee Tree Rd., PO Box 537, Frankfort, KY 40602-0537. Phone: (502) 564-8300. Original Kentucky state and county records.

Filson Club Library, 1310 S. 3rd St., Louisville, KY 40208. Phone: (502) 635-5083. Like another archives for Kentucky. Best for original manuscripts for early Kentucky history, including genealogy. They specialize in Ohio River traffic and migrations, including steamboats.

Virginia Historical Society Library, 428 North Blvd., PO Box 7311, Richmond, VA 23221-0311. Phone: (804) 358-4901. As a former county of Virginia, many of the earliest records of Kentucky can be found here, not in Kentucky. Original county records, militia lists, bounty lands, tax lists, poll lists, genealogies, newspapers, family Bibles.

Mary Ball Washington Museum and Library, Route 3, Old Jail Bldg., Old Clerks Office Bldg., and Lancaster House, PO Box 97, Lancaster, VA 22503-0097. Phone: (804) 462-7280. A name index resides in this little library taken from virtually every history book published on Virginia and Kentucky.

Brayton Collection, Santa Cruz Public Library, 224 Church St., Santa Cruz, CA 95060-3873. Phone: (408) 429-3530. Genealogical equivalent to the Draper Collection, but bigger, and with a better index. Collection is mostly compiled genealogies of Kentucky, Tennessee, the Carolinas, and Virginia.

Kentucky Library, Western Kentucky University, 1 Big Red Way, Bowling Green, KY 42101-3576. Phone: (502) 745-6258. A great repository for historical resources, including southern history, oral history, biographies, early settlers, and Shakers.

King Library, University of Kentucky, Lexington, KY 40506-0039. Phone: (606) 257-3801. Appalachian collection, newspapers, and historical manuscripts relating to Kentucky.

Daviess County Public Library, 450 Griffith Ave., Owensboro, KY 42301. Phone: (502) 684-0211. Genealogy and Local History Department houses one of the best genealogy collections in Kentucky.

Kentucky Genealogical Society Library, PO Box 153, Frankfort, KY 40602. Phone: (502) 875-4452. A very good collection of statewide Kentucky records, guides, censuses, cemeteries, biographies, family folders, periodicals, indexes, and more.

Draper Papers (See Wisconsin: State Historical Society of Wisconsin).

Durrett Collection (See Illinois: University of Chicago Library).

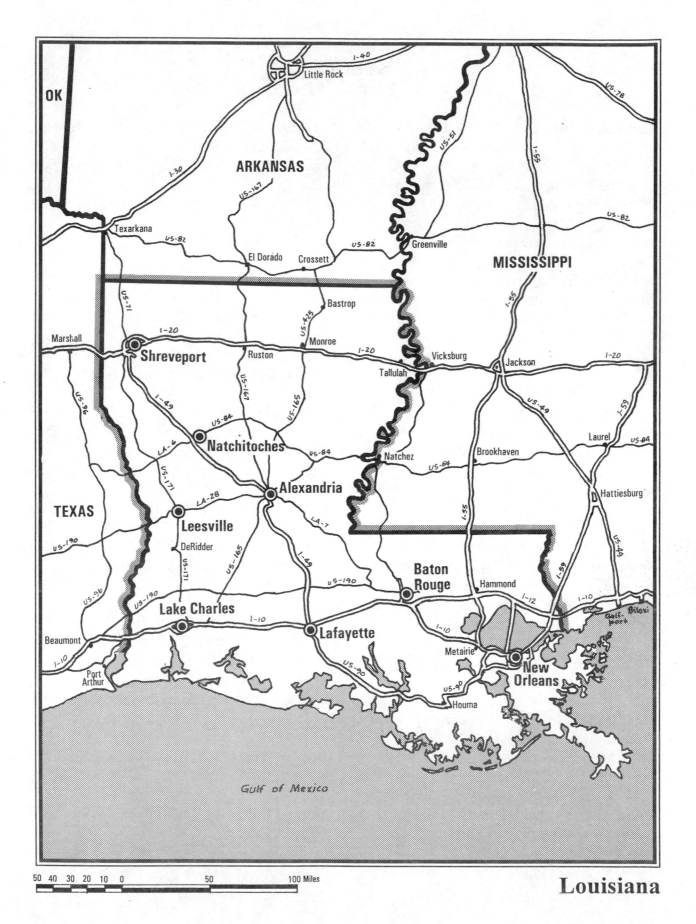

Louisiana

Louisiana

Louisiana State Archives, 3851 Essen Ln., PO Box 94125, Capitol Station, Baton Rouge, LA 70804-9125. Phone: (504) 922-1207. Records for all Louisiana parishes. Great surname indexes. Special collections for Louisiana Confederates (Rebel Collection), lumber industry, and oral histories. Without a doubt, this is the best genealogy research facility in Louisiana.

Howard-Tilton Memorial Library, Tulane University, 7001 Freret St., New Orleans, LA 70118-5682. Phone: (504) 865-5131. A large genealogical collection, perhaps the best overall genealogy collection in the state.

New Orleans Public Library, Genealogy Department, 219 Loyola Ave., New Orleans, LA 70140-1016. Phone: (504) 596-2550. U.S. immigration records, newspapers, and genealogies. The best book collection related to genealogy in the state.

Historic New Orleans Collection Library, 533 Royal St., New Orleans, LA 70130. Phone: (504) 523-4662. Records relate to life in New Orleans, Louisiana, and the lower Mississippi Valley. Records include many references dating back to the French era.

Alexandria Historical and Genealogical Library, 503 Washington St., Alexandria, LA 71301. Phone: (318) 487-8556. A huge regional library with books, periodicals, family folders, and many indexes to statewide records. This is a primary research center for Louisiana.

Shreve Memorial Library, 424 Texas, PO Box 21523, Shreveport, LA 71120. Phone: (318) 226-5897. A regional library, with good coverage of the Ark-La-Tex region. The genealogy collection is mostly books and periodicals, but the coverage is excellent.

Calcasieu Parish Public Library, 301 W. Claude St., Lake Charles, LA 70605. Phone: (318) 475-8792. Louisiana history and genealogy collection is large. Parish histories, genealogies, surname folders, periodicals, and microfilms.

Dupre Library, University of Southwestern Louisiana, 302 E. St. Mary Blvd., USL Box 4019, Lafayette, LA 70503-2038. Phone: (318) 482-6030. Great collections relating to Acadian/Cajun and Creole families, folklore, local history, Louisiana history, and more.

Natchitoches Genealogical and Historical Association, 2nd Floor, Parish Courthouse, PO Box 1349, Natchitoches, LA 71458-1349. Phone: (318) 357-2235. The "French Archives" has records dating back to the early 1700's, with an index kept by the Parish Court Clerk. As a stop on the road to Texas, Natchitoches was a place where many Texas people left marks.

Vernon Parish Library, 1401 Nolan Trace, Leesville, LA 71446-0310. Phone: (318) 239-2027. This library has a very large Louisiana history and genealogy collection.

East Baton Rouge Public Library, 7711 Goodwood Blvd., Baton Rouge, LA 70806. Phone: (504) 231-3750. This regional library has one of the best genealogy collections in the state, with many books, periodicals, vertical files, family folders, genealogies, biographies, newspapers, obituaries, and many microfilms and printed sources for Louisiana genealogy.

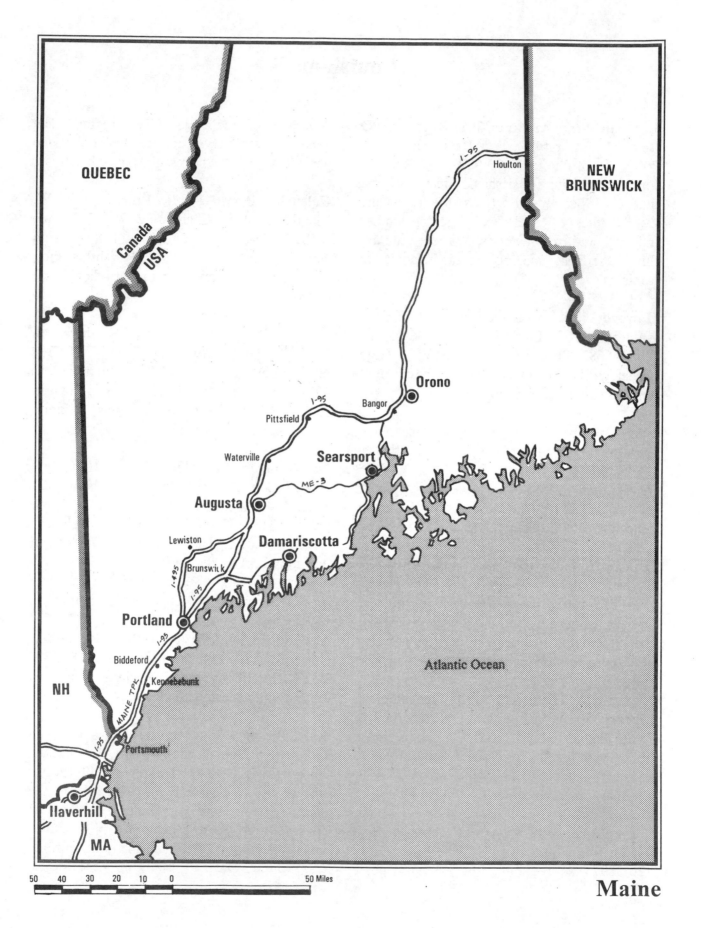

QUEBEC

Canada
USA

NEW
BRUNSWICK

I-95   Houlton

Orono

I-95   Bangor

Pittsfield

Waterville

Searsport

ME-3

Augusta

Lewiston

Damariscotta

I-495

Brunswick

I-95

Portland

I-95

Biddeford

MAINE TPK.

Kennebunk

NH

I-95

Portsmouth

Atlantic Ocean

Haverhill

MA

50 40 30 20 10 0   50 Miles

Maine

Maine

Maine State Library, State House Station #64, Augusta, ME 04333-0064. Phone: (207) 287-5600. History, genealogy, towns, counties, Indians, boundaries, rivers, maps, oral history, and government documents. The best in Maine.

Maine State Archives, State House Station #84, Augusta, ME 04333-0084. Phone: (207) 287-5795. Original records from all Maine counties and towns.

Massachusetts Archives, 220 Morrissey Blvd., Boston, MA 02125. Phone: (617) 727-2816. Since Maine was formerly part of Massachusetts, most of the records up to 1820 can be found in Massachusetts. Perhaps the starting point for genealogists is the "Massachusetts Archives Index" formerly called the "Colonial Index". The name of virtually every immigrant to New England during the colonial period can be found in this index.

New England Historic Genealogical Society Library, 101 Newbury St., Boston, MA 02116-3087. Phone: (617) 536-5740. Early Maine families are covered in great detail. The library has many unpublished family histories for Maine people. In addition, the book collection for Maine town and county histories is very large and useful.

Massachusetts Historical Society Library, 1154 Boylston St., Boston, MA 02215-3695. Phone: (617) 536-1608. An excellent collection of historical materials related to Maine.

American Antiquarian Society Library, 185 Salisbury St., Worcester, MA 01609-1634. Phone: (508) 755-5221. Many Maine records, including vital records, early newspapers, and town histories. One of the best genealogy resources centers in America.

Fogler Library, University of Maine, 5729 Fogler Library, Orono, ME 04469. Phone: (207) 581-1661. Excellent collections of early Maine settlers, fisheries, Acadians, ships, and shippers.

Maine Historical Society Library, 485 Congress St., Portland, ME 04101. Phone: (207) 774-1822. Great collection for genealogists.

Penobscot Maritime Museum, Stephen Phillips Memorial Library, PO Box 498, Searsport, ME 04974. Phone: (207) 548-2529. An important biographical index of Maine people, plus shippers, ship registers, logbooks, journals, and more.

Haverhill Public Library, Genealogy Department, 99 Main St., Haverhill, MA 01830-5092. Phone: (978) 373-1586. A collection of New England genealogies, town histories, and more. The size of this library's genealogical collection ranks with the best in New England. Its collection of New England source materials is larger than several better known New England repositories.

Skidompha Library, Main St., PO Box 70, Damariscotta, ME 04543. Phone: (207) 563-5513. Genealogy and Local History collection is outstanding.

National Archives, Northeast Region, (Boston), Frederick C. Murphy Federal Center, 380 Trapelo Road, Waltham, MA 02154. Phone: (781) 647-8104. All U.S. federal censuses, 1790-1920, all soundex indexes, and all printed census indexes.

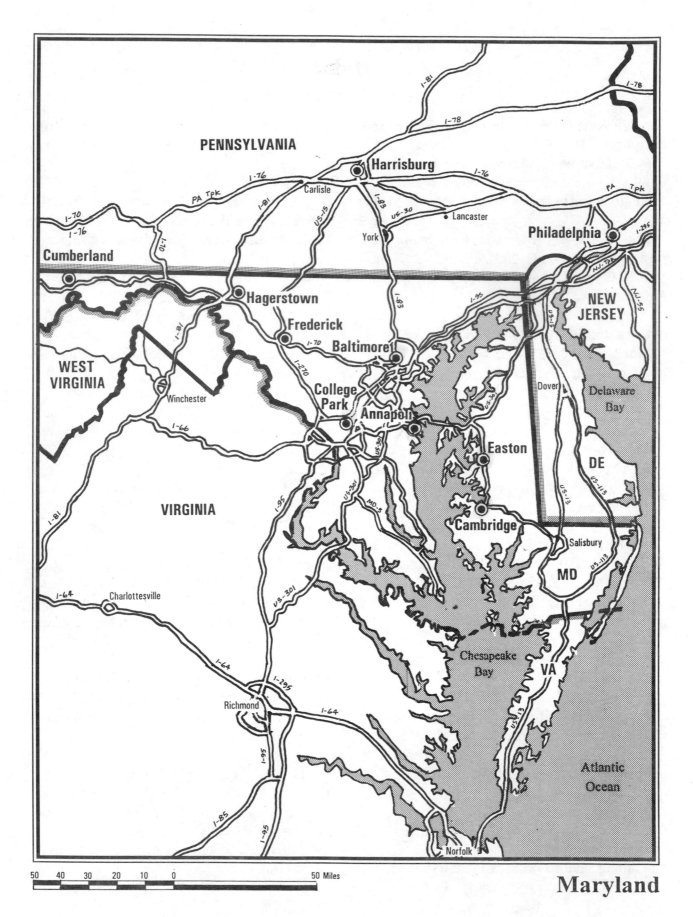

Maryland

Maryland

Maryland State Archives, 350 Rowe Blvd., Annapolis, MD 21401. Phone: (410) 974-3914. The Maryland State Archives has the most complete collection of historical documents of any of the 13 original colonies. Included in its holdings are colonial and state records dating back to the founding of the colony in 1634, county probate, land, and court records, church records and many other records relevant to genealogical research. There are over 130 major card indexes to Maryland deeds, land records, and early settlers. In addition, newspapers, county records, church records, family, and business records are included in the major indexes. This is the premier resource center for locating Maryland settlers. All of the original documents are beautifully preserved. Plan to stay awhile. It may take three full days just to check the indexes.

Maryland Historical Society, 201 W. Monument St., Baltimore, MD 21201. Phone: (410) 685-3750. Like another state archives. Largest genealogical book collection for Maryland plus family Bibles, newspapers, biographies, genealogies, and much more.

Sat 9—5
11—5 Sunday

Enoch Pratt Free Library, 400 Cathedral St., Baltimore, MD 21201-4484. Phone: (410) 396-5430. Excellent collection of local, county, and state of Maryland records. *Sat 10—5 p no Sunday*

McKeldin Library, University of Maryland, College Park, MD 20742. Phone: (301) 454-5977. Large Maryland historical collection.

Pennsylvania Historical and Museum Commission, Reference Library, William Penn Memorial Museum and Archives Building, 3rd and N Streets, PO Box 1026, Harrisburg, PA 17108-1026. Phone: (717) 783-9898. Colonial records include many references to Maryland settlements.

Allegany County Library, 31 Washington St., Cumberland, MD 21502-2981. Phone: (301) 777-1200. Western Maryland historical collection, genealogy, local history.

Frederick County Public Library, 110 E. Patrick, Frederick, MD 21701-5630. Phone: (301) 694-1613. Maryland history, genealogy, and more.

Washington County Free Library, 100 S. Potomac St., Hagerstown, MD 21740. Phone: (301) 739-3250. Western Maryland room is the place for genealogists. Collection has published histories, oral histories, books, periodicals, family folders, and more.

Talbot County Free Library, 100 W. Dover St., Easton, MD 21601-2617. Phone: (410) 822-1626. Many Maryland Eastern Shore and Delaware historical references.

Dorchester County Public Library, 303 Gay St., Cambridge, MD 21613. Phone: (410) 228-7331. Many Maryland Eastern Shore and Delaware historical references.

Historical Society of Pennsylvania Library, 1300 Locust St., Philadelphia, PA 19107-5699. Phone: (215) 732-6200. Original records of early Quakers, Germans, Scotch-Irish, and other colonial settlers in Penn's colonies. An excellent place to locate early settlers in Pennsylvania, New Jersey, and Maryland.

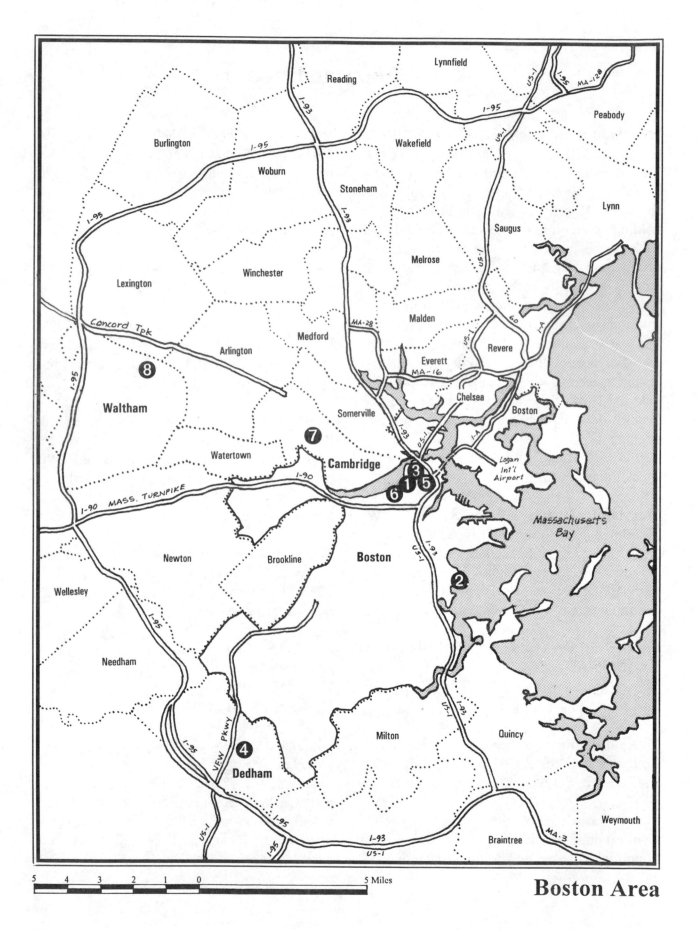

Boston Area

Massachusetts (Boston Area)

Note: Numbers indicate the location of each facility on the map

❶ **New England Historic Genealogical Society Library**, 101 Newbury St., Boston, MA 02116-3087. Phone: (617) 536-5740. In addition to the best overall collection for New England, the library has an excellent collection of Canadian genealogy materials, plus a sizeable collection for Great Britain, Ireland, and continental Europe. The Manuscript Collection is available to members exclusively and contains diaries and letters; account books and business papers; church and town records; sermons, maps, wills and deeds; unpublished New England town and family genealogies; the papers of many of the region's best genealogists, deposited here since the 1850's; and family photographs.

❷ **Massachusetts Archives**, 220 Morrissey Blvd., Boston, MA 02125. Phone: (617) 727-2816. Perhaps the starting point for genealogists is the "Massachusetts Archives Index," formerly called the "Colonial Index". The names of nearly all immigrants to New England during the colonial period can be found in this index.

❸ **Massachusetts Historical Society Library**, 1154 Boylston St., Boston, MA 02215-3695. Phone: (617) 536-1608. An excellent collection of historical materials: original town records, newspapers, and genealogies. Virtually all records are unique and not repeats of materials at the New England Historic Genealogical Society library.

❹ **Dedham Historical Society Library**, 612 High St., PO Box 215, Dedham, MA 02027. Phone: (781) 326-1385. Outstanding collection of original manuscripts, including deeds, vitals, and town records for the 15 towns created from old Dedham (from south and west of Boston to the Plymouth Colony bounds and as far south as the Rhode Island boundary).

❺ **State Library of Massachusetts**, 341 State House, Boston, MA 02133. Phone: (617) 727-2590. Published books, periodicals, and town histories.

❻ **Boston Public Library**, Genealogy and Local History, 700 Boylston St., Boston, MA 02117-0286. Phone: (617) 536-5400. New England city directories, town and county histories, published histories, and genealogies.

❼ **Houghton Library**, Harvard University, Cambridge, MA 02138. Phone: (617) 495-2441. Rare books and manuscripts, early and illuminated manuscripts, literary manuscripts of all periods and many countries with particular concentration on American (New England), British, and Continental authors; historical archives, including publishing history, and political and missionary archives; philosophy and music; Indic, Turkish, Arabic, Persian, and Syriac manuscripts; papyri; drawings and paintings; and artifacts. The collection of primary historical documents is unmatched by any other American repository in sheer volume.

❽ **National Archives**, Northeast Region, Frederick C. Murphy Federal Center, 380 Trapelo Road, Waltham, MA 02154. Phone: (781) 647-8104. All U.S. censuses and all printed census indexes.

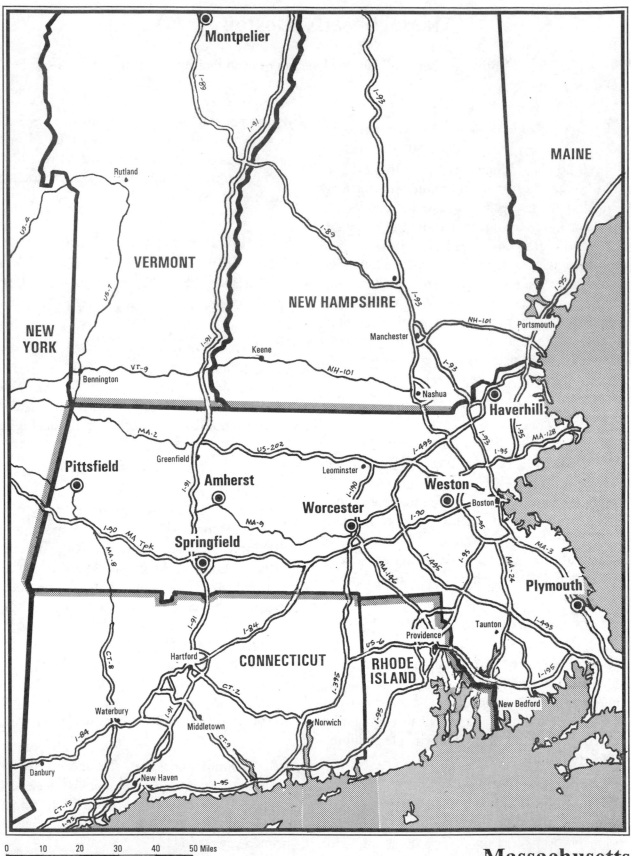

Montpelier

I-88-1

I-91

I-93

MAINE

Rutland

US-4

US-7

VERMONT

NEW HAMPSHIRE

I-89

I-93

NH-101

Portsmouth

Manchester

I-93

NEW YORK

I-91

Keene

NH-101

VT-9

Bennington

Nashua

MA-2

Haverhill

US-202

I-495

I-93

I-95

MA-128

Pittsfield

Greenfield

Leominster

Weston

I-91

Amherst

I-190

Boston

Worcester

MA-9

I-90

I-90

MA-Tpk

Springfield

I-495

I-95

MA-3

MA-8

MA-146

MA-24

Plymouth

I-91

I-84

Taunton

I-495

CT-8

Hartford

CONNECTICUT

US-6

Providence

RHODE
ISLAND

CT-2

New Bedford

I-395

I-95

I-195

Waterbury

I-91

Middletown

Norwich

I-84

CT-9

Danbury

New Haven

I-95

CT-15

I-95

| 0 | 10 | 20 | 30 | 40 | 50 Miles |

Massachusetts

Massachusetts (except Boston)

American Antiquarian Society Library, 185 Salisbury St., Worcester, MA 01609-1634. Phone: (508) 755-5221. This library is best known for its newspaper collection.For the U.S. alone, there are over 18,000 bound volumes of newspapers from 1704-1820 representing the single largest collection of extant newspapers for that period. One of the top U.S. facilities.

Haverhill Public Library, Genealogy Department, 99 Main St., Haverhill, MA 01830-5092. Phone: (978) 373-1586. The size of this library's genealogical collection ranks with the best in New England, with a surprisingly large number of original manuscripts, books, periodicals, and surname folders.

Jones Library, Inc., 43 Amity Street, Amherst, MA 01002-2285. Phone: (413) 256-4090. The Boltwood Collection of Local History and Genealogy has New England genealogies, family folders, and more.

National Archives, Northeast Region (Pittsfield), 100 Dan Fox Dr., Pittsfield, MA 01201. Phone: (413) 445-6885. All federal censuses, 1790-1920, plus all soundex and printed censuses.

Berkshire Athenaeum, Pittsfield Public Library, 1 Wendell Ave., Pittsfield, MA 01201-6385. Phone: (413) 499-9480. For western Massachusetts this is the place to go. Newspapers, published resources, family histories, and much more.

University of Massachusetts at Amherst Library, Box 34710, Amherst, MA 01003. Phone: (413) 545-0284. Huge collection of biographies, genealogies, and histories never published, plus church, business, fraternal, insurance, and manufacturing records.

Connecticut Valley Historical Museum Library, 220 State St., Springfield, MA 01103. Phone: (413) 263-6800. An important resource center for identifying Massachusetts people who migrated west. Vital records, land records, and probates from many New England counties and towns.

Onondaga Historical Association Library, 311 Montgomery St., Syracuse, NY 13202-2098. Phone: (315) 428-1862. This resource center has the largest family folder collection in the northeast with as many as 10,000 families identified. Many of the people identified were from Massachusetts.

Plymouth Public Library, 132 South St., Plymouth, MA 02360. Phone: (508) 830-4250. Virtually all published records of early Massachusetts families can be found here.

Vermont Historical Society Library, General Services Center - Reference Research, Drawer 33, Montpelier, VT 05633-7601. Phone: (802) 828-3286. The name index to Massachusetts people in this resource center is very comprehensive.

Family History Center, 150 Brown St., Weston, MA 02193 (LDS Chapel). Phone: (781) 235-2164. This is the largest New England Family History Center. The collection includes published records from virtually every town and county of New England, plus social histories, vital records, published indexes, and family histories. This is a unique collection and not well known by genealogists in New England, yet the facility is open to the public. Well staffed. Call for hours of operation.

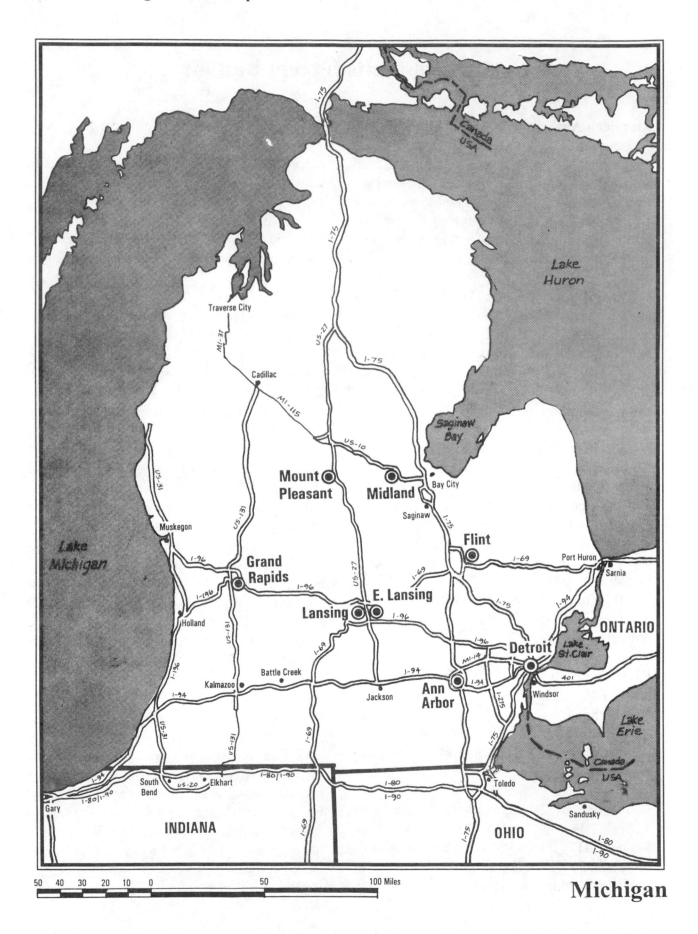

Traverse City

Cadillac

MI-37

US-27

I-75

Canada USA

Lake Huron

Saginaw Bay

Mount Pleasant ● ● **Midland** Bay City

MI-115

US-10

Muskegon

US-31

US-131

Saginaw

Grand Rapids ● I-96

I-96

Lake Michigan

I-96

E. Lansing

Lansing ● ● I-96

Flint ●

I-69

Port Huron

Sarnia

ONTARIO

Holland ●

US-131

US-27

I-69

I-75

I-94

Lake St.Clair

Detroit ●

MI-14

I-96

I-275

Windsor

401

Battle Creek ●

Kalmazoo ●

I-94

US-131

MI-96

I-69

Jackson ●

Ann Arbor ●

I-94

I-94

Lake Erie

US-31

US-131

South Bend ●

US-20

Elkhart ●

I-80/I-90

I-94

I-69

I-80

I-80

I-90

Canada USA

Toledo

Gary

I-80/I-90

INDIANA

I-69

I-75

OHIO

Sandusky ●

I-80

I-90

50 40 30 20 10 0   50   100 Miles

Michigan

Michigan

Library of Michigan, Genealogy Department, 717 W. Allegan Ave., PO Box 30007, Lansing, MI 48909. Phone: (517)373-1580. A very complete genealogy collection with periodicals, county histories, family histories for Michigan, Ohio, New York, and New England states.

Michigan State Archives, 717 W. Allegan Ave., Lansing, MI 48918. Phone: (517) 373-1408. Every county of Michigan represented with vitals, deeds, probates, etc., plus early state records, land records, licenses, notaries, probates, and departmental records.

Detroit Public Library, 5201 Woodward Ave., Detroit, MI 48202. Phone: (313) 833-1000. Home of the Burton Historical Collection and the Detroit Society for Genealogical Research. Many unpublished family histories, research aids, such as indexes and guides to cemeteries, and obituaries. A large family folder collection and a very good newspaper collection.

Michigan Historical Collection, Bentley Historical Library, University of Michigan, 1150 Beal Ave., Ann Arbor, MI 48109-2113. Phone: (313) 764-3482. A huge manuscript library with many unpublished histories, biographies, travel, and newspapers.

Historical Society of Michigan, 2117 Washtenaw, Ann Arbor, MI 48104. Phone: (313) 769-1828. County records found no where else, plus genealogies, Bibles, cemetery records, newspapers, obituaries, and more.

Michigan State University Library, 100 Library, East Lansing, MI 48824-1048. Phone: (517) 355-2344. Great manuscript collection, newspapers, unpublished works on pioneers, loggers, early settlers, and more.

Flint Public Library, 1026 E. Kearsley St., Flint, MI 48502-1923. Phone: (810) 232-7111. Books, periodicals, family folders, with published references to all of Michigan. The library also has many references to the Upper Midwest, New England, and Ontario, Canada.

Grand Rapids Public Library, 60 Library Plaza N.E., Grand Rapids, MI 49503-3093. Phone: (616) 456-3600. Very good genealogy collection. Perhaps more unpublished family histories than any other library in Michigan. The genealogy library has actively solicited families histories for many years.

Grace Dow Memorial Library, 1710 W. St. Andrews Dr., Midland, MI 48640. Phone: (517) 837-3430. A small library, but with good indexes. Many sources to the earliest settlers coming to Michigan via Saginaw Bay.

Park Library, Central Michigan University, 207 Park Library, Mount Pleasant, MI 48859. Phone: (517) 774-3500. Family folders, published family genealogies, periodicals, newspapers, published court records, and Native American records. A little known facility, with lots of potential for finding Michigan ancestors.

The National Archives of Canada, 395 Wellington St.,Ottawa, ON K1A 0N3, Canada. Phone: (613) 992-6534. Many of the important records relating to Michigan immigrants are here, including land, military, estate, tax lists, and church records. This facility is open 24 hours, seven days a week.

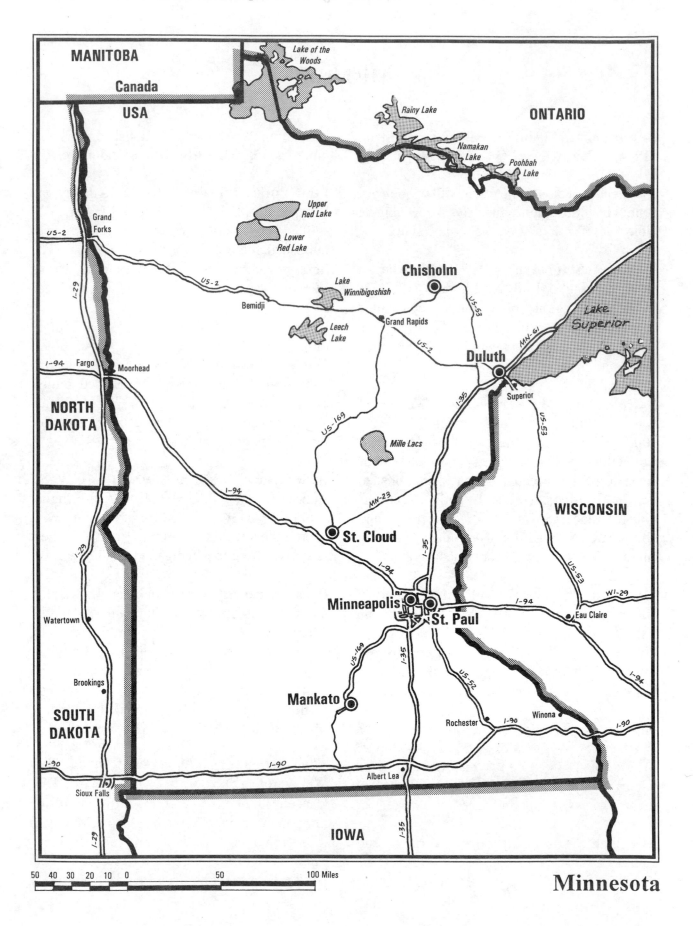

MANITOBA

Canada

USA

ONTARIO

Lake of the
Woods

Rainy Lake

Namakan
Lake

Poohbah
Lake

US-2

Grand
Forks

I-29

Upper
Red Lake

Lower
Red Lake

US-2

Bemidji

Lake
Winnibigoshish

Chisholm

Lake
Superior

US-53

Leech
Lake

Grand Rapids

US-2

MN-61

Duluth

I-94

Fargo

Moorhead

Superior

NORTH
DAKOTA

US-169

I-35

US-53

Mille Lacs

I-94

MN-23

WISCONSIN

St. Cloud

I-35

US-53

I-29

WI-29

Minneapolis

I-94

Eau Claire

St. Paul

Watertown

US-169

I-35

US-52

I-94

Brookings

Mankato

Winona

SOUTH
DAKOTA

Rochester

I-90

I-90

I-90

I-90

Albert Lea

Sioux Falls

IOWA

I-29

I-35

50 40 30 20 10 0   50   100 Miles

Minnesota

Minnesota

Minnesota History Center, Historical Society of Minnesota, 345 Kellogg Blvd., W., St. Paul, MN 55102-1906. Phone: (612) 296-6980. Great genealogy collection, histories, biographies, and newspapers. The indexes to the collection makes this facility a great place to start for Minnesota people. The genealogies are numerous for the many ethnic groups that peopled Minnesota including Swedes, Norwegians, Danes, Germans, and Native Americans. This facility acts as the state archives for Minnesota and includes many original state and county records.

Wilson Library, University of Minnesota, 309 19ᵗʰ Ave. S., Minneapolis, MN 55455-0414. Phone: (612) 624-4520. Special collections. A great historical manuscript collection, newspapers, business and church records, books, periodicals, maps, and government documents.

Immigration History Research Center, 826 Berry St., St. Paul, MN 55114. Phone: (612) 627-4208. An outstanding research facility with many records relating to the European immigrants to Minnesota. Heavy on the Czechs, Poles, Byelorussians, Carpath-Rusins, Finns, Creeks, Italians, Russians, plus more on the Albanians, Armenians, Bulgarians, Croatians, Estonians, Hungarians, Jews of eastern Europe, Latvians, Lithuanians, Macedonians, Romanians, Serbs, Slavs, and Ukrainians. There are many indexes to individuals represented in these ethnic groups.

Central Minnesota Historical Center Library, St. Cloud State University, 720 4ᵗʰ Ave. S., St. Cloud, MN 56301. Phone: (320) 255-3254. Like another state archives for Minnesota. Original manuscripts, family folders, diaries, journals, area newspapers, land ownership maps, genealogies, and histories.

Northeast Minnesota Historical Center, University of Minnesota, 10 University Dr., Duluth, MN 55812. Phone: (218) 726-8526. Many county records, denomination records, histories, family folders, books, and periodicals. A very good research facility, primarily for northeast Minnesota, but with good coverage for the Great Lakes region.

Iron Range Research Center, PO Box 392, Hwy 169, Chisholm, MN 55719. Phone: (218) 254-3325. Located in the historic mining region of Minnesota, this archives has many records relating to the people who came to work the mines. Name indexes to early immigrants, settlers, and ethnic groups coming to Minnesota.

Southern Minnesota Historical Center, Mankato State University, Mankato, MN 56001. Phone: (507) 389-1029. Periodicals, family folders, cemeteries, obituaries, manuscripts, documents, newspapers, histories, genealogies, and more.

Stearns County Historical Society Library, 235 33ʳᵈ Ave. S., PO Box 702, St. Cloud, MN 56302-0702. Phone: (320) 253-8424. A county facility, but with a statewide and U.S. scope. Many references to the lowlanders of western Europe: Luxembourgers, Belgians, southern French, and Hollanders. The collection has great indexes to the early settlers.

Minnesota Genealogical Society Library, PO Box 16069, St. Paul, MN 55116-0069. Phone: (612) 645-3671. Many ethnic resources, how-to books, periodicals, and family surname folders. The society has compiled many indexes to court records, cemeteries, and county histories. (The Library is moving to another location in 1998).

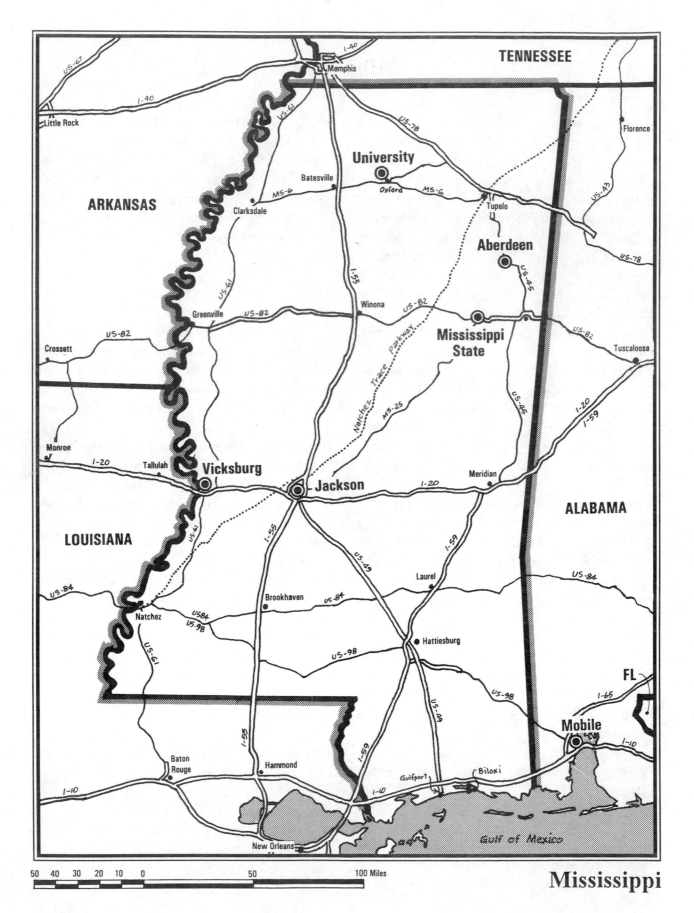

TENNESSEE

ARKANSAS

Little Rock

US-67

I-40

US-61

Memphis

I-40

US-78

Florence

US-43

Batesville

University

Oxford

MS-6

MS-6

Tupelo

Clarksdale

US-78

Aberdeen

US-45

US-82

Greenville

US-82

Winona

US-82

Mississippi State

US-82

Tuscaloosa

Crossett

US-82

Natchez Trace Parkway

MS-25

US-45

I-20

I-59

Monroe

I-20

Tallulah

Vicksburg

I-55

Jackson

I-20

Meridian

ALABAMA

LOUISIANA

US-61

I-55

US-49

I-59

Laurel

US-84

US-84

Brookhaven

US-84

Natchez

US-84

US-98

Hattiesburg

US-98

FL

US-61

US-98

I-65

US-98

US-49

Mobile

I-10

I-55

I-59

Baton Rouge

Hammond

Gulfport

Biloxi

I-10

I-10

New Orleans

Gulf of Mexico

50 40 30 20 10 0   50   100 Miles

Mississippi

Mississippi

Mississippi State Department of History and Archives, Archives and Library Division, 100 S. State St., PO Box 571, Jackson, MS 39201. Phone: (601) 359-6850, ext. 34. All Mississippi counties represented with original records, a large newspaper collection, many genealogies, county histories, and manuscripts. This is clearly the best facility for genealogical research in Mississippi.

Evans Memorial Library, 105 N. Long St., Aberdeen, MS 39730. Phone: (601)369-4601. This is an outstanding regional library with many Mississippi references. The genealogy collection is one of the largest in the South, with a very large book collection, periodicals, family surname folders, manuscripts, microfilmed newspapers, personal and business letters, diaries, account books, and photographs, plus rare and special books from prominent Mississippians. The Mississippi Collection is a large array of books about early Mississippi. This library could be called "the Fort Wayne Library of the South."

Mississippi Historical Society Library, PO Box 571, Jackson, MS 36201. Phone: (601) 359-6850. A good genealogy collection, with many original historical manuscripts, newspapers, histories, genealogies, periodicals, and unpublished histories.

Mobile Municipal Archives, PO Box 1827, Mobile, AL 36633-1827. Phone: (334) 208-7740. Archives includes records of early Mississippi settlers, Spanish, French, Anglos, and more. Records in this facility relate to the entire Gulf Coast region, including the Florida Panhandle, Alabama, Mississippi, and Louisiana. The records are heavily concentrated to the Spanish era. There are some guides and indexes to these records; but the guides are mostly related to specific subjects, where one can find and search within records related to military, land, early censuses, church records, business records, or family histories.

McCardle Library, Old Court House Museum, Vicksburg and Warren County Historical Society, 1008 Cherry St., Vicksburg, MS 39180. Phone: (601) 636-0741. Regional and local genealogy for early Mississippi families, military records, and more.

Mitchell Memorial Library, Mississippi State University, PO Box 9570, Mississippi State, MS 39762. Phone: (601) 325-3060. Books, manuscripts, maps, biographies, and genealogies.

University of Mississippi Library, Special Collections, University, MS 38677. Phone: (601) 232-5855. An excellent collection of records relating to Mississippi including early logging, early settlers, oral histories, manuscripts, histories, and more.

Barker Texas History Center, UT Center for American History, SRH 2-101, Collections Deposit Library, University of Texas, Austin, TX 78713-7330. Phone: (512) 463-5460. This library is the keeper of *The Natchez Trace Collection*, formerly in Natchez, Mississippi, but removed to Texas. The records contain manuscripts, legal documents, photographs, maps, pamphlets, military officers, lawyers, steamboat operators, slaves, homemakers, merchants, and physicians documenting life and culture in the Lower Mississippi Valley from the late 1600's.

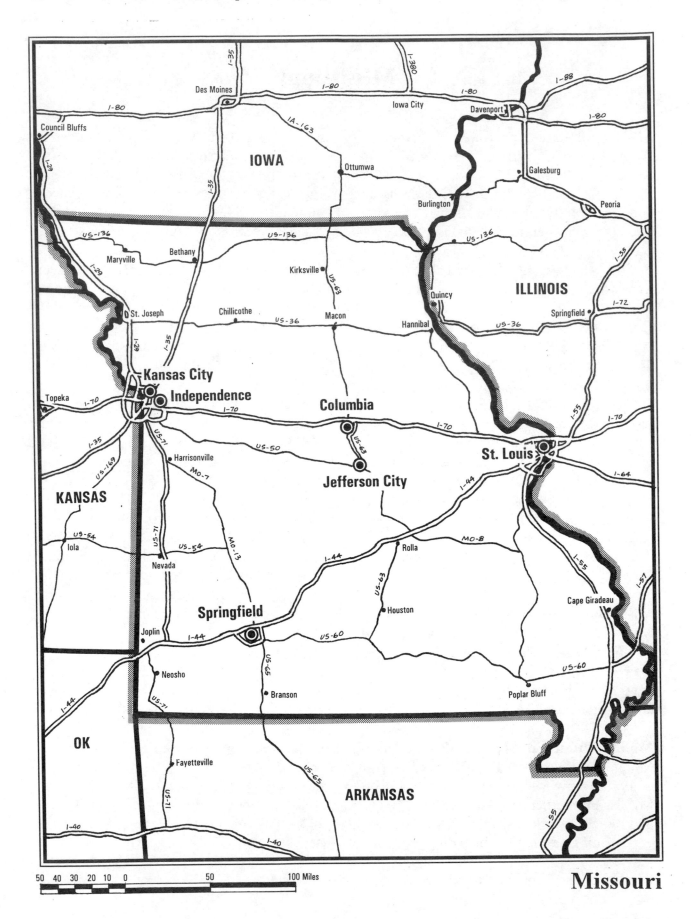

Missouri

Missouri

Mid-Continent Public Library, North Independence Branch, 15616 E. Highway 24, Independence, MO 64050. Phone: (816) 252-0950. This is one of only three public libraries in America which has a complete set of all federal censuses, 1790-1920, all soundex and printed census indexes, plus many other National Archives microfilms of interest to genealogists. In addition, state and local records from Missouri and the surrounding states are well represented. All in all, this is one of the most complete genealogy resource centers in America.

Missouri Historical Society, Library and Archives, 225 S. Skinker Blvd., PO Box 11940, St. Louis, MO 631112-0040. Phone: (314) 746-4500. An excellent collection of early Missouri records, plus many other records relating to people who came through Missouri via Illinois.

Missouri State Archives, PO Box 778, Jefferson City, MO 65102. Phone: (573) 751-3280. All Missouri counties represented with microfilm of original county records. This facility is "user-friendly" to genealogists.

State Historical Society of Missouri Library, 1020 Lowry St., Columbia, MO 65201-7298. Phone: (573) 882-7083. A good genealogy collection with many historic Missouri manuscripts and reference materials.

Special Collections, Kansas City Public Library, 311 E. 12th, Kansas City, MO 64106-2454. This is an outstanding genealogy collection, with many references to the Missouri Valley, biographies, periodicals, genealogies, and more.

Saint Louis Public Library, 1301 Olive St. Louis, MO 63103-2389. Phone: (314) 539-0385. Excellent collection of census records, early newspapers, biographies, genealogies. A premier library for Missouri research, rivaling any other in the state.

Harrison County Historical Museum, Hughes Research Center Library, Marshall, TX 75670. Phone: (903) 938-2680. This archives has the key to locating many early Missouri families. Marshall, Texas, was a Confederate center during the Civil War, and for a time, served as the capital of the Confederate State of Missouri. An outstanding collection of family folders, letters, diaries, journals, and surname lists.

National Archives, Central Plains Region, 2312 E. Bannister Rd., Kansas City, MO 64131. Phone: (816) 926-6920. All microfilm for U.S. federal censuses, 1790-1920, plus all soundex indexes and virtually all printed statewide census indexes. Historical records date from 1821 to the 1980's, including maps, naturalization records, immigration records, military and pension records, adoptions, divorces, federal land records, and more. Among subjects of local interest are frontier and territorial history; American Indians native to the Northern Great Plains, and court cases.

Springfield-Greene County Library, 397 East Central, Springfield, MO 65802. Phone: (417) 837-5000, and **Ozarks Genealogical Society Library**, 534 West Catalpa, Springfield, MO 65802. Phone: (417) 831-2773. Both libraries have substantial genealogy coverage of southern Missouri.

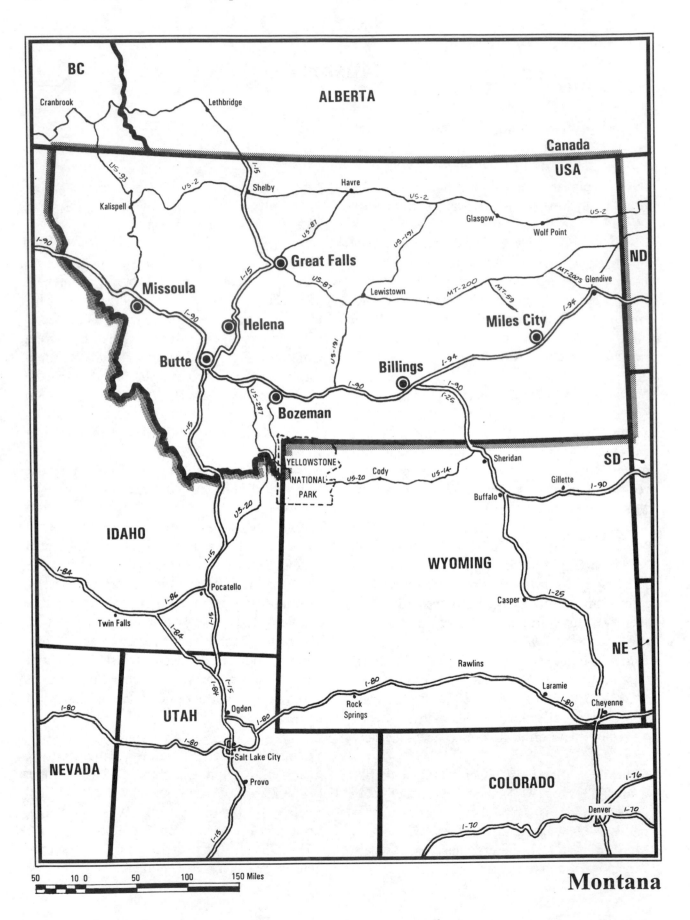

Montana

Montana

Montana Historical Society Library and Archives, 225 N. Roberts, Helena, MT 59620. Phone: (406) 444-2681. A good historical collection for early Montana people, range cattle industry 1860-1945, newspapers, George Armstrong Custer, Yellowstone Park, and more. This is the official state archives for Montana, and all counties are represented with original documents, histories, and historical publications. This is the starting place for Montana genealogy.

Maureen and Mike Mansfield Library, University of Montana, Missoula, MT 59812. Phone: (406) 243-6800. An excellent collection of Montana history, lumber industry and other Montana businesses, oral histories, and U.S. documents.

Montana State Library, 1515 E. 6th St., Helena, MT 59620. Phone: (406) 444-3004. Good historical collection for early Montana. Large book library and many microfilms of newspapers and historical references.

Montana State University Library, Special Collections, Bozeman, MT 59717. Phone: (406) 994-3119. A good historical and genealogy collection. Montana histories and town and county histories. A good source for records relating to the early mining industry and the Montana ranching industry.

Parmly Billings Library, 510 N. Broadway, Billings, MT 59101. Phone: (406) 657-8257. Montana histories, county histories, genealogies. One of the rare public libraries with set of early law digests for the entire U.S. (Indexes and abstracts of state court cases). This library's collection covers Eastern Montana in great detail, plus it has many records for the Dakotas and Wyoming. It also has many indexes to biographies, cemeteries, and other records of genealogical value.

Bancroft Library, University of California, Berkeley, CA 94720. Phone: (415) 642-3781. The "Bancroft Collection" is outstanding for early settlers, early trails, stagecoaches, miners, histories, etc. This library has many historical documents relating to early Montana.

Great Falls Genealogical Society Library, Paris Gibson Square, 1400 1st Ave., N. - Room 30, Great Falls, MT 59401-3299. Phone: (406) 727-3922. A huge reference library with statewide newspapers, indexes to records, family folders, cemeteries, and county records.

Miles City Public Library, 1 S. 10th St., Miles City, MT 59301. Phone: (406) 232-1496. Montana histories, biographies, censuses, genealogies, and more.

Eastern Montana College Library, 1500 N. 30th St., Billings, MT 59101-0298. Phone: (406) 657-2011. Special collections related to Battle of Little Big Horn and 7th U.S. Cavalry, books, manuscripts, Billings and Yellowstone County and Eastern Montana history, western history, maps, and U.S. documents.

Butte-Silver Bow Public Library, 226 W. Broadway St., Butte, MT 59701. Phone: (406) 723-8262. Old and rare books, Montana histories, biographies, county histories, and genealogies.

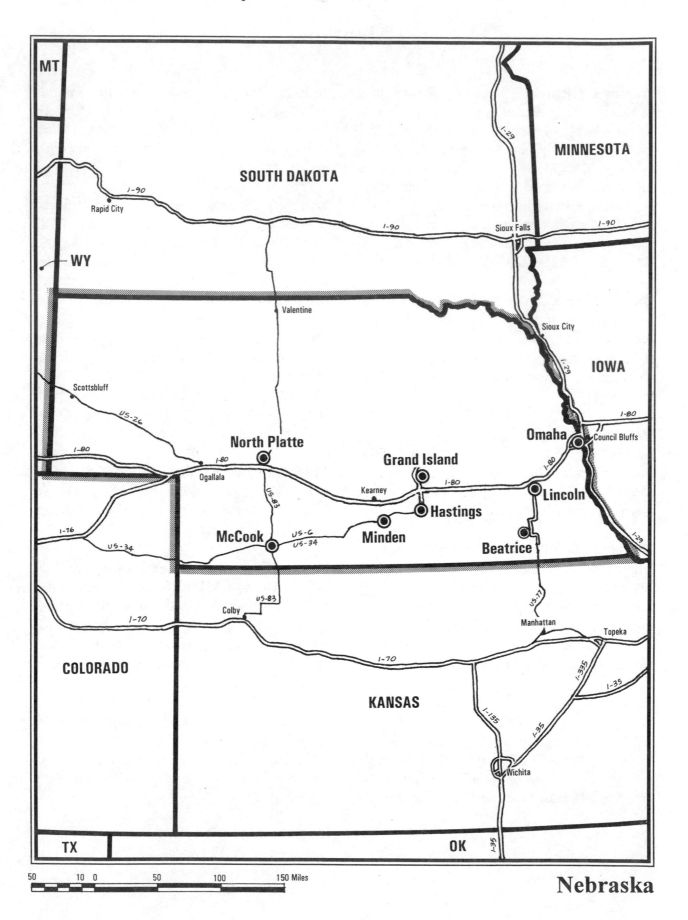

Nebraska

Nebraska

Nebraska State Historical Society Library, Department of Reference Services, 1500 R St., PO Box 82554, Lincoln, NE 68501. Phone: (402) 471-3270. The best collection of genealogical materials in the state, including biographies, Nebraska histories, cemetery transcriptions, federal censuses, territorial and state censuses (1854-1869), periodicals, church records, statewide directories, state and local histories, copies of federal land tract books, railroads, military records, maps, gazetteers, microfilmed index to all Nebraska naturalizations before 1906, and over 20,000 microfilms of Nebraska newspapers,

Love Memorial Library, Special Collections, University of Nebraska, Lincoln, NE 68588-0410. Phone: (402) 472-2526. Many manuscripts and histories not in Historical Society, plus special collections on Czechoslovakians, Latvians, 20th Century Russians, folklore, military history, and plains materials.

Bancroft Library, University of California, Berkeley, CA 94720. Phone: (415) 642-3781. The "Bancroft Collection" is outstanding for early settlers, early trails, stagecoaches, miners, histories, etc. This library has many historical documents relating to early Nebraska.

Omaha Public Library, Genealogy Department, 215 S. 15th St., Omaha, NE 68102-1004. Phone: (402) 444-4800. A good genealogy collection. Books, periodicals, and name indexes.

North Platte Public Library, 120 W. 4th St., North Platte, NE 69101. Phone: (308) 535-8036. A good genealogy collection. Books, periodicals, and genealogies.

Edith Abbott Memorial Library, 211 N. Washington, Grand Island, NE 68801. Phone: (308) 385-5333. A good genealogy collection.

National Archives, Central Plains Region, 2312 E. Bannister Rd., Kansas City, MO 64131. Phone: (816) 926-6920. All microfilm for U.S. federal censuses, 1790-1920, plus all soundex indexes and virtually all printed statewide census indexes. Included are Federal court records (1855-1960) from Nebraska, such as bankruptcies, divorces, criminal and civil court cases, land records, immigrations, and naturalizations.

South Central Nebraska Genealogical Society Library, Route 2, Box 57, Minden, NE 68959. A trail-oriented library with numerous references to Oregon-Mormon-California trails.

Southeast Nebraska Genealogical Society Library, PO Box 562, Beatrice, NE 68310. A good genealogy library. Books, periodicals, family folders, and microfilm resources.

Von Riesen Library, McCook Community College, 1205 E. 3rd St., McCook, NE 69001-2631. Phone: (308) 345-6303, ext. 41. Basic genealogy collection of books, microfilms, and periodicals. A regional collection of genealogical materials deposited by the local genealogical society, added to the college sources.

Adams County Historical Society Archives, 1330 N. Burlington Ave., PO Box 102, Hastings, NE 68902. Phone: (402) 463-5838. Newspapers, church records, records of the dust bowl years, oral histories, and many references to the Oregon-California-Mormon trail.

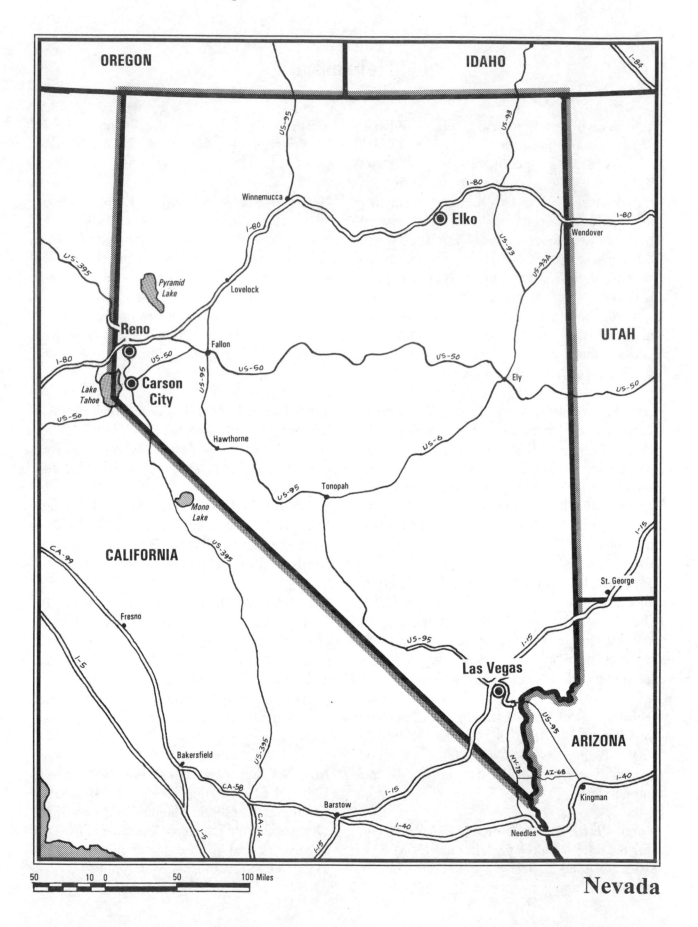

Nevada

Nevada

Nevada State Library and Archives, 100 N. Stewart Street, Carson City, NV 89701. Phone: (702) 687-8313. Territorial and state censuses, 1855-1875, territorial court records, 1855-1862, prison inmate case files from 1863, orphan homes from 1870, auto license plate registrations, adjutant general's military records, Secretary of State's civil records, Nevada newspapers and indexes, and many original state and countywide records, such as tax records and vital records.

Nevada Historical Society, Museum-Research Library, 1650 N. Virginia St., Reno, NV 89503-1799. Phone: (702) 688-1190. A good genealogy collection. Like another state archives. The society publishes a great periodical which is well indexed. Collection includes newspapers, biographies, records of early pioneers, mining industry, gambling industry, Native Americans, and more.

Gretchell Library, University of Nevada, Reno, NV 89557-0004. Phone: (702) 784-6533. Largest collection of historical materials related to Nevada's early pioneers, settlers, miners, and Native Americans.

Dickinson Library, University of Nevada, 4505 Maryland Pkwy, Las Vegas, NV 89154-0001. Phone: (702) 895-3286. A very large research library with many books, periodicals, indexes, newspapers, biographies, and histories. The collection is large enough to qualify as the state library for Nevada.

Bancroft Library, University of California, Berkeley, CA 94720. Phone: (415) 642-3781. The "Bancroft Collection" is outstanding for early settlers, early trails, stagecoaches, miners, histories, etc. This library has many historical documents relating to early Nevada.

National Archives, Pacific Region (San Francisco), 1000 Commodore Dr., San Bruno, CA 94066. Phone: (650) 876-9001. All U.S. federal censuses, 1790-1920, plus all soundex and printed indexes. Records from Northern California counties, plus Nevada (except Clark County) including federal court records, bankruptcies, divorces, immigration and naturalization records, and federal court case files, mining claims, land records, and many documents relating to early Nevada history.

National Archives, Pacific Region (Laguna Niguel), 24000 Avilla Rd., first floor, east entrance, Laguna Niguel, CA 92677. Phone: (714) 360-2626. All microfilm for U.S. federal censuses, 1790-1920, plus all soundex and printed census indexes. Federal court and other federal records from Southern California counties and Clark County, Nevada, are maintained at this facility. Federal court records, bankruptcies, divorces, immigration and naturalization records, and federal court case files, mining claims, land records, and many documents relating to early Nevada history.

Northeastern Nevada Historical Society Library, 1515 Idaho St., Elko, NV 89801. Phone: (702) 738-3418. Newspaper, manuscripts, diaries, journals. Heavy on mining, including claims, mining company records, and miners. This facility is also an excellent Basque research center, with many references to the early Basque sheep herders in the West, plus good indexes to the records. Biographies, obituaries, local burials, and more.

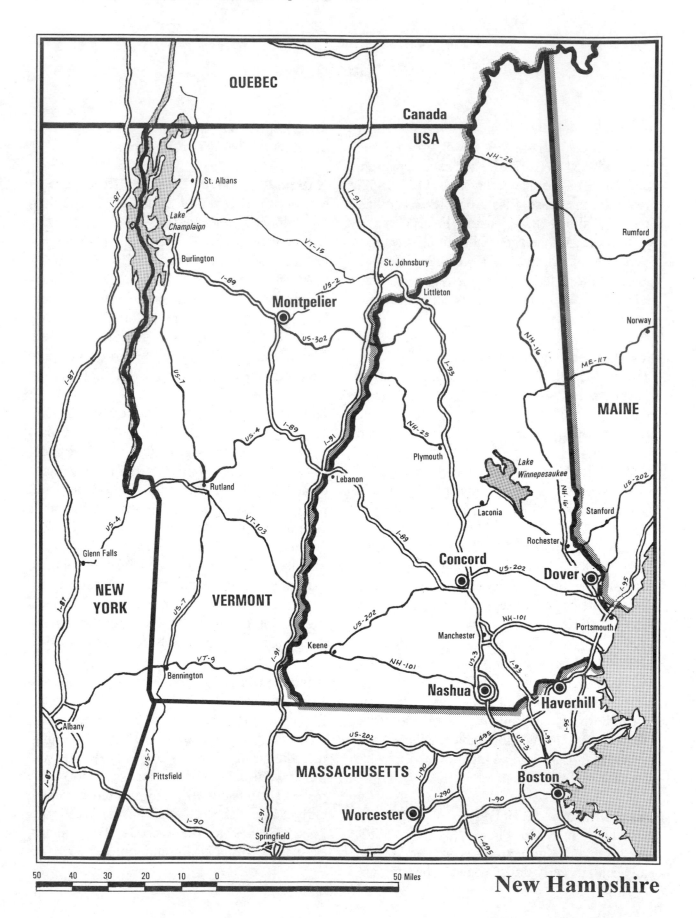

New Hampshire

New Hampshire

New Hampshire Historical Society Library, 30 Park St., Concord, NH 03301-6384. Phone: (603) 225-3381. Clearly the best genealogy collection in the state. New Hampshire history, town and county histories and genealogies, newspapers, church records, provincial deeds, 1640-1770, broadsides, and maps. The library has over 5,000 genealogies, most of which are unpublished. They also have over 4,000 biographical works and over 1,000 state, county, and town maps, plus some 200 manuscript volumes of church records from all parts of New Hampshire. Over 100 towns are represented with cemetery records. There are 800,000 pages of New Hampshire newspapers and a unique card index of some 30,000 "New Hampshire Notables" gathered from such sources as biographical dictionaries, local histories, and obituaries. This is the place to start genealogical research for a New Hampshire ancestor.

Records and Archives Library, State of New Hampshire, Department of State, 71 S. Fruit St., Concord, NH 03301-2410. Phone: (603) 271-2236. Original town and state records.

New Hampshire State Library, 20 Park St., Concord, NH 03301. Phone: (603) 271-2392. Virtually every published history and genealogy for New Hampshire.

American Antiquarian Society Library, 185 Salisbury St., Worcester, MA 01609-1634. Phone: (508) 755-5221. Many New Hampshire records, including vital records, early newspapers, and town histories.

Vermont Historical Society Library, 109 State St., Montpelier, VT 05609. Phone: (802) 828-2291. An outstanding source for locating early New Hampshire people. (Vermont was claimed by New Hampshire and New York until Vermont became a state in 1792).

Haverhill Public Library, Genealogy Department, 99 Main St., Haverhill, MA 01830-5092. Phone: (978) 373-1586. A collection of New England genealogies, town histories, and more. Located very near the New Hampshire border, this library has an outstanding collection of early New Hampshire families in its genealogical department.

Massachusetts Archives of the Commonwealth, 220 Morrissey Blvd., Boston, MA 02125. Phone: (617) 727-2816. The "Massachusetts Archives Index" formerly called the "Colonial Index" has the name of virtually every immigrant to New England during the colonial period, including those who came to New Hampshire.

Nashua Public Library, 2 Court St., Nashua, NH 03060. Phone: (603) 594-3412. Nice genealogy collection in one room. Upper New England books, family folders, cemeteries, obituaries, and documents.

Dover Public Library, 73 Locust St., Dover, NH 03820. Phone: (603) 742-6050. New Hampshire genealogical materials, with many family genealogies, printed works, indexes, cemeteries, obituaries, biographies. An excellent collection for genealogical research.

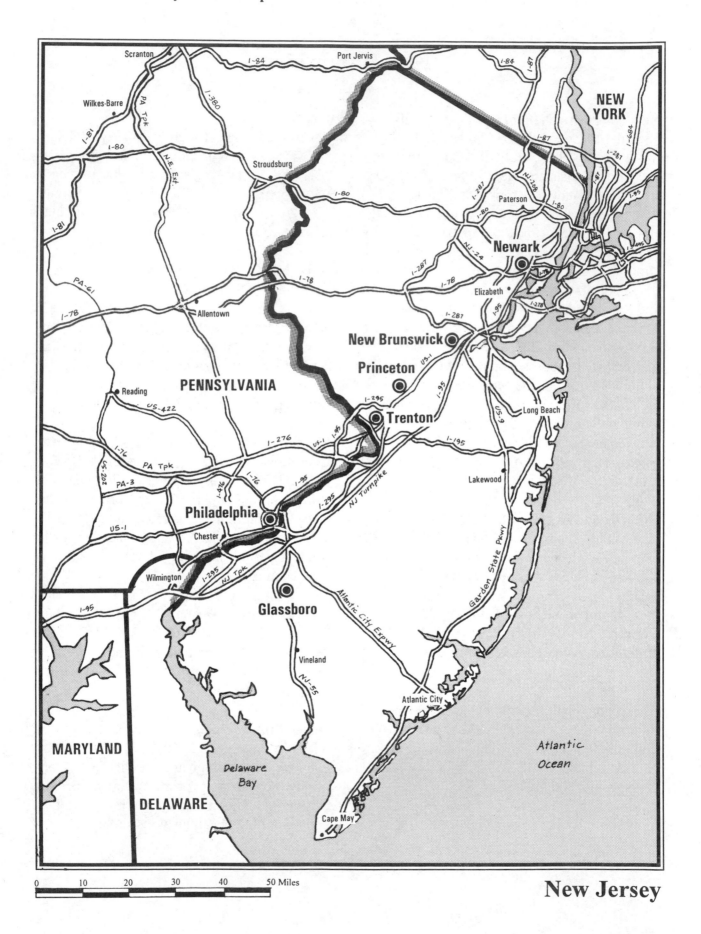

New Jersey

New Jersey

Alexander Library, Special Collections and Archives, Rutgers University, 169 College Ave., New Brunswick, NJ 08903. Ph: (201) 932-7129. Among the collection are numerous original letters and documents by noted Americans and foreigners, early New Jersey town records, original manuscripts, diaries from 1746 to 1986, books printed before 1500, seventeenth-century tracts promoting settlements in New Jersey and elsewhere, first and signed editions of many famous literary works, historical maps and newspapers, early prints and photographs, almanacs, and museum objects. The collection also contains the records gathered by the New Jersey Genealogical Society and the Daughters of the American Revolution. The Rutgers genealogical collection is also significant, including biographies, histories, genealogies, family folders, Bibles, census, and specialized indexes to records, cemetery inscriptions, and extensive notes and compilations by professional genealogists, many of whom have spent a lifetime studying the state's early families. This facility is the first place a researcher should visit for New Jersey genealogical research.

New Jersey State Archives, 185 West State Street-Level 2, New Jersey State Library Building, Trenton, NJ 08625-0307. Phone: (609) 292-6260. Original records include petitions to the governor and legislature; New Jersey wills, 1670-1900; supreme and chancery court records, 1680-1850; state census records, 1855-1915; 20th century election returns; birth records, 1848-1923; marriage and death records, 1848-1940; tax ratables, 1772-1822; railroad, turnpike, and canal maps and records; colonial deeds, 1660s-1780s; and military records dating from the American Revolution.

New Jersey Historical Society Library, 52 Park Place, Newark, NJ 07102. Phone: (973) 596-8500. This facility has as many genealogical and biographical materials as the state archives in Trenton.

New Jersey State Library, 185 W. State St., Level 4 (State Street side) CN 520, PO Box 520, Trenton, NJ 08625-0520. Phone: (609) 292-6274. The genealogical collection consists mainly of published records including guides, indexes, how-to books, periodicals, family genealogies and printed family records, with a major emphasis on New Jersey and surrounding states. Also included are New Jersey county and local histories, New Jersey city directories and New Jersey printed maps and atlases.

Firestone Library, Princeton University Library, 1 Washington Rd., Princeton, NJ 08544-2098. Phone: (609) 258-3180. Manuscript collection is huge, plus histories, biographies, and more.

Savitz Library, Glassboro State University, Center St. and College Ave., Glassboro, NJ 08028-1995. Phone: (609) 863-6102. Delaware Valley history, including Quaker genealogies for virtually every Quaker line in every county of New Jersey. If you have Quaker ancestors from New Jersey, this library is a must.

Historical Society of Pennsylvania Library, 1300 Locust St., Philadelphia, PA 19107-5699. Phone: (215) 732-6200. Original records of early Quakers, Germans, Scotch-Irish, and other colonial settlers in Penn's colonies. An excellent place to locate early settlers in Pennsylvania, New Jersey, and Delaware.

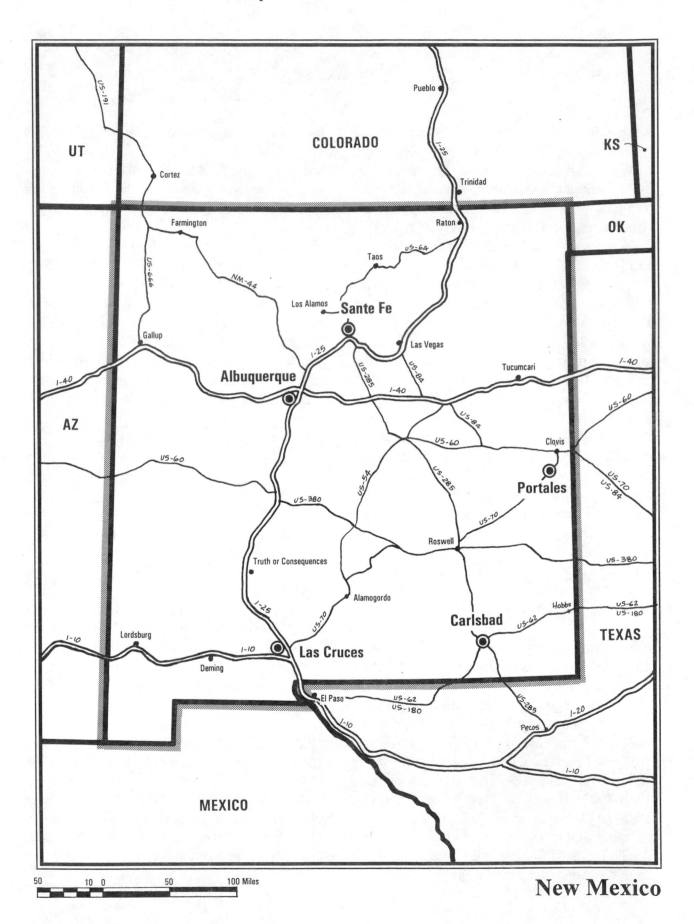

New Mexico

New Mexico

New Mexico State Archives, 1205 Camino Carlos Rey, Santa Fe, NM 87505. Phone: (505) 476-7908. Original territorial, state, and county records. New Mexico's best facility for genealogical research mainly for the original state and county records available.

Albuquerque Public Library, Special Collections (Genealogy), 423 Central Ave., Albuquerque, NM 87102. Phone: (505) 768-5140. One building devoted to genealogy and southwestern history. A great facility with a great genealogy collection, including New Mexico vital records, histories, biographies, periodicals, and family folders.

Museum of New Mexico, History Library, 110 Washington Ave., PO Box 2087, Sante Fe, NM 87504-2087. Phone: (505) 827-6451. Manuscripts, newspapers, rare books, maps, colonial Spanish and Mexican papers, Native Indians, photo archives — collection is as large as that of the State Archives.

Bancroft Library, University of California, Berkeley, CA 94720. Phone: (415) 642-3781. The "Bancroft Collection" is outstanding for early settlers, early trails, stagecoaches, miners, histories, etc., including many references to New Mexico people.

Zimmerman Library, Special Collections, University of New Mexico, Albuquerque, NM 87131. Phone: (505) 277-4241. Large manuscript collection, heavy on Spanish, early Mexican, censuses, early Anglo records.

New Mexico State Library, 325 Don Gaspar, Santa Fe, NM 87501. Phone: (505) 827-3800. Largest book library in the state. Government documents, maps, periodicals, biographies, and genealogies. Moving to new building, late 1998.

Carlsbad Public Library, 101 S. Halagueno, Carlsbad, NM 88220. Phone: (505) 885-6776. Great genealogical collection. The impact of snowbird genealogy hobbyists traveling to New Mexico every winter means that this library acquires numerous genealogies from all over the country. The genealogy collection is strong.

Portales Public Library, 218 S. Ave. B, Portales, NM 88130. Phone: (505)356-3940. A nice genealogy library, with many references for New Mexico and out of state locations, including Texas, Tennessee, and Arkansas materials. The collection includes genealogies, periodicals, family folders, and more.

Spanish History Museum Library, 2221 Lead S.E., Albuquerque, NM 87106. Best surname folder collection for Hispanic families in the U.S. An outstanding collection of coats-of-arms histories for Spanish families and a good collection of general Hispanic materials.

Southeast New Mexico Historical Society Library, 101 S. Halagueno, Carlsbad, NM 88220. Phone: (505) 885-6776. A good regional historical library with many manuscripts, histories, journals, plus indexes to the earliest pioneers, cattlemen, range wars, and mining industry.

Rio Grande Historical Collection, New Mexico State University Library, PO Box 3006, Las Cruces, NM 88003-3006. Phone: (505) 646-1508. Spanish records from the 1500's, identifying many families living along the old El Camino Real (the Spanish mission road of the Rio Grande Valley, from the Sangre de Christo Mountains of Colorado to the Gulf of Mexico.)

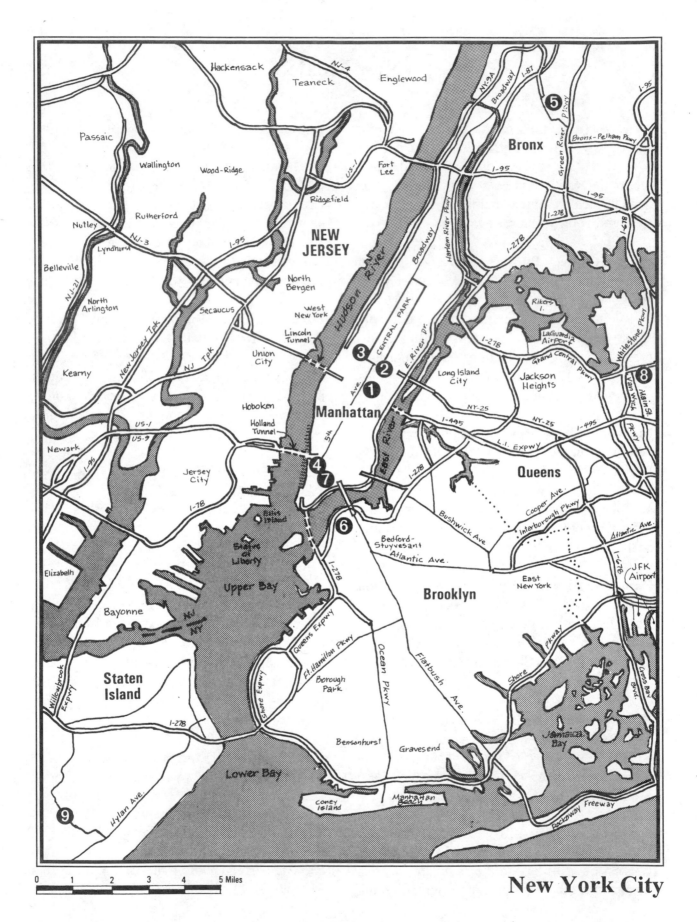

New York City

New York City

Note: Numbers indicate the location of each facility on the map)

❶ **New York Public Library**, 5th Ave. and 42nd St., New York City, NY 10018. Phone: (212) 930-0800. Genealogy and local history collection is one of the best in the U.S., plus biographies, histories, manuscripts, Revolutionary War soldiers' papers, Irish in America, and more.

❷ **New York Genealogical and Biographical Society Library**, 122 E. 58th St., New York City, NY 10022-1939. Very large collection of unpublished manuscript genealogies, and much more.

❷ **Holland Society of New York Library**, 122 E. 58th St., New York, NY 10022. Phone: (212) 758-1675. Early Dutch records, but this facility has many records for other ethnic groups for the entire Atlantic coast region.

❷ **Huguenot Society of America Library**, 122 E. 58th St., New York, NY 10022. Phone: (212) 755-0592. Largest Huguenot collection outside of London. Starting with the 1600's, records from France, Belgium, Holland, England, and Colonial America.

❸ **New York Historical Society Library**, 170 Central Park W., New York City, NY 10024-5194. Phone: (212) 873-3400. Largest manuscript collection in New York, with tax, newspapers, town and village records, colonial records, biographies, genealogies.

❹ **National Archives, Northeast Region**, 201 Varick St., 12th floor, New York, NY 10014. All microfilm for U.S. federal censuses, 1790-1920, plus all soundex and printed statewide census indexes. The archival collection includes federal records from New Jersey, New York, Puerto Rico, and the Virgin Islands.

❺ **Bronx County Historical Society Library**, 3309 Bainbridge Ave., Bronx, NY 10467. Phone: (718) 881-8900. Huge manuscript collection, biographical files, family folders, and documents, obituaries, cemetery files, city directories, marriages, and more.

❻ **Brooklyn Historical Society Library**, 128 Pierrepont St., Brooklyn, NY 11201. Phone: (718) 624-0890. Manuscripts for all of New York City and Long Island. Many records of New England immigrants to Suffolk County, New York. Great indexes to family names.

❼ **New York City Municipal Reference and Research Center**, 31 Chambers St., New York, NY 10007. Phone: (212) 788-8590. New York street name origins, city council reference, serials, and books. This agency publishes a government guide to New York City, indicating the type of records held by various city departments.

❽ **Queens Historical Society Library**, 143-35 37th Ave., Flushing, NY 11354. Phone: (718) 939-0647. A large facility, with many indexes to biographical and historical references.

❾ **Staten Island Historical Society Library**, 441 Clarke Ave., Staten Island, NY 10306. Phone: (718) 351-1611. The place for Staten Island research. With lots of New York immigrants moving through Staten Island, the records apply to many migratory families.

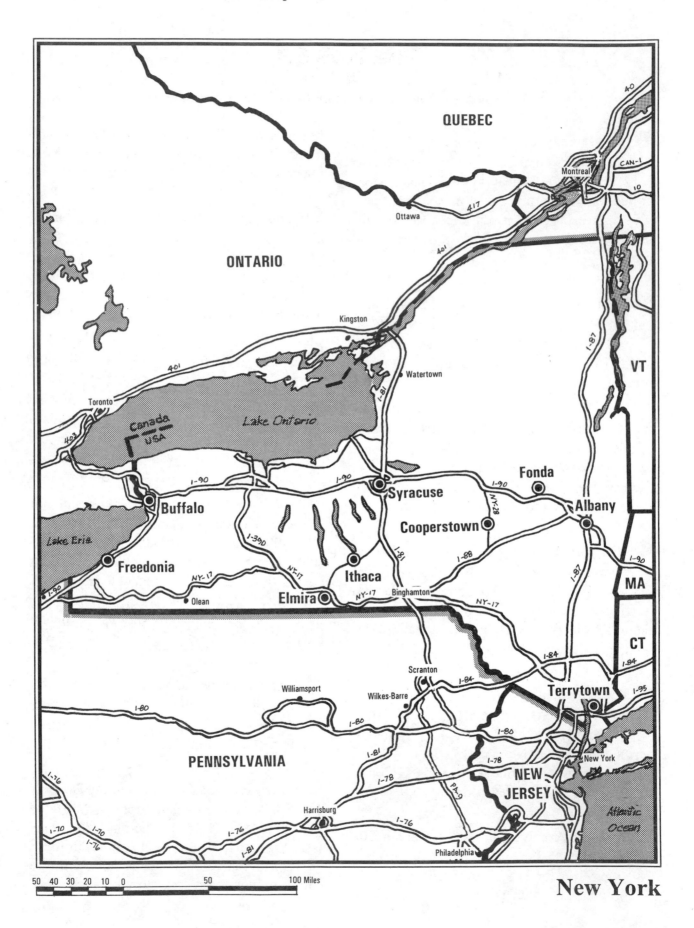

New York

New York (except New York City)

New York State Archives, Cultural Education Center, Room 11D40, Albany, NY 12230. Phone: (518) 474-8955. Original colonial, state, county, and town records, militia, census, vital records, genealogies, and many manuscripts.

New York State Library, Cultural Education Center, Empire State Plaza, Albany, NY 12230. Phone: (518) 474-5355. Same building as the state archives. Great genealogy collection for New York. Good indexes to publications, documents, manuscripts, and genealogical reference materials.

Research Center, Onondaga Historical Association, 311 Montgomery St., Syracuse, NY 13202-2098. Phone: (315) 428-1862. The best collection of family folders on the East coast with over 10,000 folders, making this library a great place for research in New York.

Albany Institute of History and Art, McKinney Library, 125 Washington Ave., Albany, NY 12210. Phone: (518) 463-4478. The facility has the best indexes to the original records from the early 1600's including references to families moving into old Albany county during the colonial period.

Montgomery County Department of History and Archives Library, Old Courthouse, PO Box 1500, Fonda, NY 12068-1500. Phone: (518) 853-8187. As an early New York county which covered much of upstate New York, the records in this facility are unique. They have an extensive genealogical collection.

Reed Library, State University of New York, Fredonia, NY 14063. Phone: (716) 673-3184. For Western New York and a large part of Northwestern Pennsylvania, the Holland Land Company granted patents of land to individuals. Most of the original land records are in this facility.

Cornell University Library, Ithaca, NY 14853-5301. Phone: (607) 255-3530. Rare books and manuscripts collection is outstanding. Cornell publishes the best research guides to New York counties.

Research Library, New York State Historical Association, Lake Road, PO Box 800, Cooperstown, NY 13326. Phone: (607) 547-1470. A collection nearly as large as that of the New York Historical Society in New York City but with better coverage for upstate New York. Manuscripts, periodicals, family folders, books, maps, biographies, county histories, and more.

Buffalo and Erie County Public Library, Lafayette Square, Buffalo, NY 14203-1887. Phone: (716) 858-8900. A good genealogy collection. Good indexes. Many biographies, family folders, county and town histories with good coverage for the entire state of New York.

Steele Memorial Library, 101 E. Church St., Elmira, NY 14901-2799. Phone: (607) 733-8602. Good indexes to biographies, genealogies, family folders, books, periodicals, and manuscripts.

Historic Hudson Valley Library, 150 White Plains Rd., Tarrytown, NY 10591. Phone: (914) 631-8200. By appointment only. Genealogists are referred to the Westchester Historical Society library in Elmsford, New York, but this library's collection includes unique references to early Hudson River migrations, steamboats, industries, culture, and more.

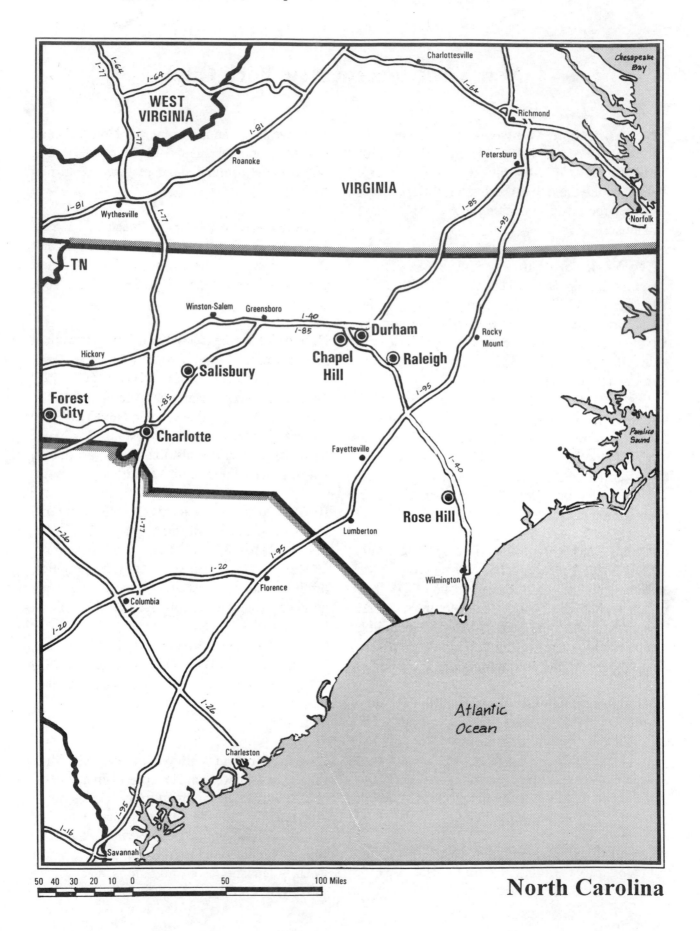

Joyner Library
@ ECTC
Greenville NC
(Pitt) Co.

North Carolina

North Carolina State Archives, 109 E. Jones St., Raleigh, NC 27601-2807. Phone: (919) 733-3952. Original manuscripts of county court records from all counties, a collection so large the archives has not been able to catalog it all.

North Carolina State Library, 109 E. Jones St., Raleigh, NC 27611. Phone: (919) 733-3270. An outstanding collection of books, periodicals, and genealogies for North Carolina.

Chattanooga-Hamilton County Bicentennial Library, 1001 Broad St., Chattanooga, TN 37402-2652. Phone: (423) 757-5310. The largest family folder file collection in the Upper South, heavy on North Carolina families.

Davis Library, University of North Carolina, CB 3900, Chapel Hill, NC 27514-8890. Phone: (919) 962-1301. North Carolina history, rare books, and the famed "Southern Historical Collection."

Perkins Library, Duke University, Durham, NC 27706. Phone: (919) 660-5870. Perhaps the largest manuscript collection in the South. Many original census records were transferred to this facility from the national archives, plus it has newspapers, county records, Bible records, journals, and much more.

Knox County Public Library, 500 W. Church St., Knoxville, TN 37902-2505. Phone: (423) 544-5750. McClung Historical Collection includes an index to early North Carolina families. There is nothing comparable to this index anywhere in North Carolina.

Rowan Public Library, 201 W. Fisher St., PO Box 4039, Salisbury, NC 28144. Phone: (704) 638-3000. Rowan county was the crossroads

of North Carolina during the colonial period, and a large central area of the present state. Many manuscripts, diaries, journals, Bibles records, family folders, and much more.

Public Library of Charlotte and Mecklenburg County, 310 N. Tryon St., Charlotte, NC 28202-2176. Phone: (704) 336-2725. Like the state archives for Southern North Carolina. Heavy emphasis on Germans, highland Scots, and Scotch-Irish immigrants to North Carolina. Many references to Quakers migrating to North Carolina from Pennsylvania. Good indexes, biographies, family folders, genealogies, and more.

Genealogical Society of Old Tryon County, U.S. Highway 74, PO Box 938, Forest City, NC 28043. Phone: (704) 248-4010. For both Carolinas, this is an excellent library for finding books, periodicals, Bible records, obituaries, biographies, indexes — mostly for pre-Civil War people.

McEachern Library of Local History, Duplin County Historical Society, 314 E. Main St., PO Box 130, Rose Hill, NC 28458. Phone: (910) 296-2180. This library has the largest collection of Scottish family folders in North America. The immigration of highland Scots to the Cape Fear River region of North Carolina is well documented. Good indexes, biographies, histories, and genealogies.

Brayton Collection, Santa Cruz Public Library, 224 Church St., Santa Cruz, CA 95060-3873. Phone: (408) 429-3533. Genealogical equivalent to the Draper Collection, but bigger, and with a better index. Collection has many compiled genealogies of early North Carolina.

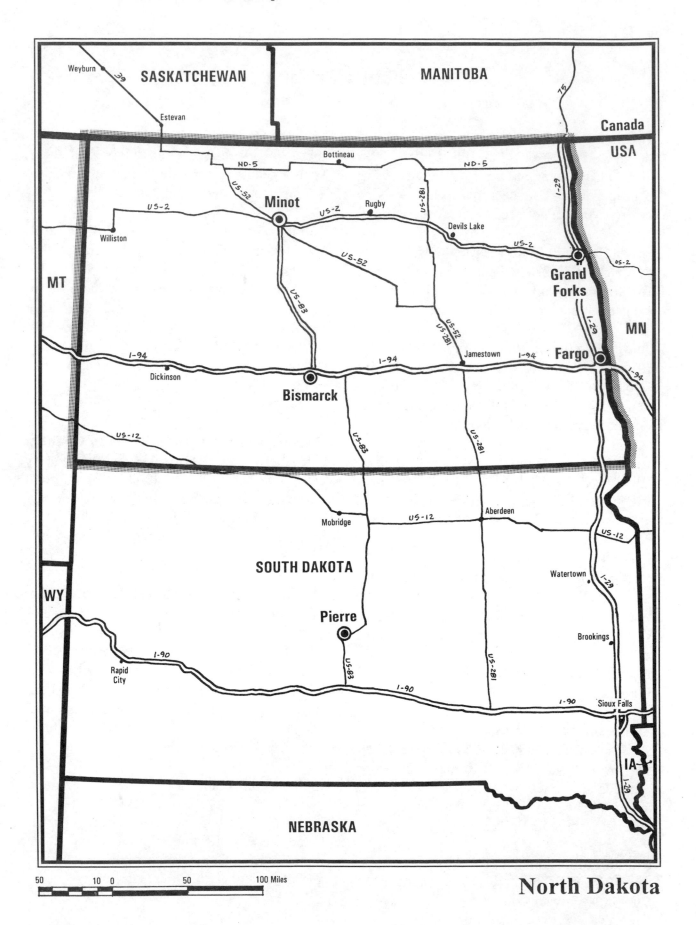

North Dakota

North Dakota

South Dakota State Historical Society, State Archives, 900 Governors Dr., Pierre, SD 57501-5070. Phone: (605) 773-3458. Original records for old Dakota Territory, including histories, biographies, homesteads, farming, and genealogies. There is more here on early North Dakota county records than can be found in the North Dakota Heritage Center.

North Dakota State University Library, PO Box 5599, Fargo, ND 58105-5599. Phone: (701) 231-8876. North Dakota history, pioneer reminiscences, bonanza farming, North Dakota biography index, historical manuscripts, photographs and book collection, and Germans from Russia Heritage collection. This library houses the **North Dakota Institute for Regional Studies**, which has many references to the earliest Dakota Territory people, trappers, farmers, cattlemen, and ethnic groups such as the Germans from Russia.

North Dakota Heritage Center, State Archives and Historical Research Library, 612 E. Boulevard Ave., Bismarck, ND 58505-0830. Phone: (701) 328-2091. Oral histories, land records, newspapers, naturalizations, a statewide death index, and records for all North Dakota counties.

North Dakota State Library, Liberty Memorial Building, Capitol Grounds, 604 E Blvd., Bismarck, ND 58505-0800. Phone: (701) 328-4622. The largest book library in the state. Wonderful for newspapers, periodicals, and reference books of all types including ethnic histories, maps, and much more.

Bismarck—Mandan Historical and Genealogical Society Library, PO Box 485, Bismarck, ND 58502. Phone: (701) 223-6273.

This is the largest genealogical society in the state, and the library is huge. A very good collection of North Dakota biographies, county histories, genealogies, family folders, and indexes. A must visit if a researcher has North Dakota ancestors.

Chester Fritz Library, University of North Dakota, PO Box 9000, Grand Forks, ND 58202-9000. Phone: (701) 777-2617. Like another state archives. North Dakota state and local histories, ethnic records, heavy on Volga German settlers in Dakota. Biographies, reference works, newspapers, and much more.

Bancroft Library, University of California, Berkeley, CA 94720. Phone: (415) 642-3781. The "Bancroft Collection" is outstanding for early settlers, early trails, stagecoaches, miners, histories, etc., including many references to North Dakota people.

Minnesota History Center, Historical Society of Minnesota, 345 Kellogg Blvd., W., St. Paul, MN 55102-1906. Phone: (612) 296-6980. Great genealogy collection, histories, biographies, and newspapers. The indexes to the collection include many references to North Dakota people including many ethnic groups that peopled North Dakota, such as the Swedes, Norwegians, Danes, and Germans.

Minot Public Library, 516 2nd Ave. S.W., Minot, ND 58701-3792. Phone: (701) 852-1045. Fine collection of genealogical materials, books, periodicals, special indexes to cemeteries, obituaries, and information on early settlers. Good coverage of people going into Canada, and people going west. The collection is a key to locating early people migrating in or out of North Dakota.

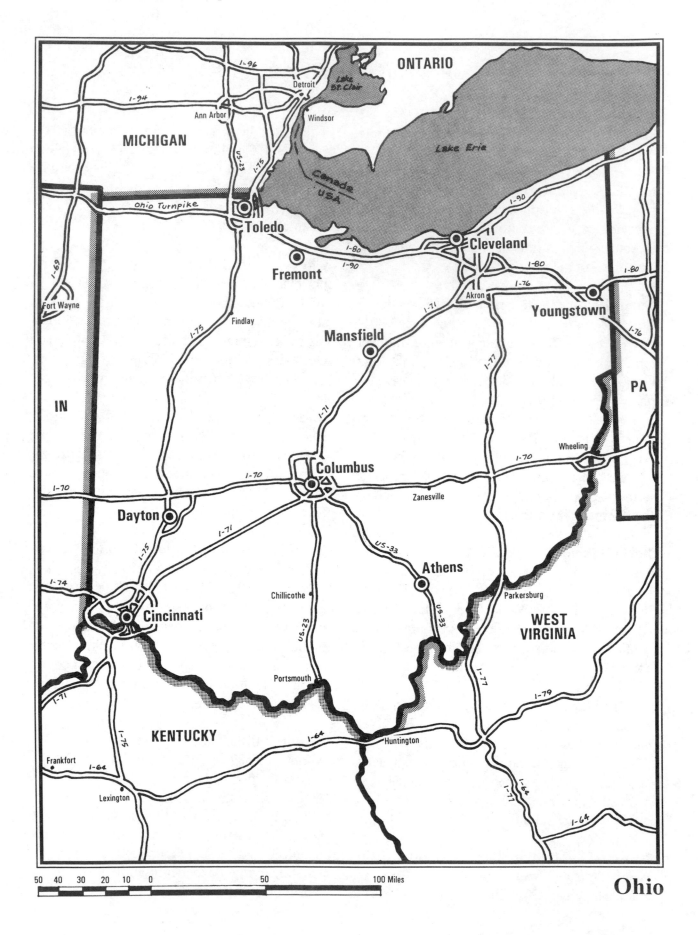

ONTARIO

MICHIGAN

Lake St. Clair

Detroit

Ann Arbor

Windsor

I-96

I-94

US-23

I-75

Lake Erie

Canada U.S.A.

Ohio Turnpike

I-90

Toledo

Fremont

I-80

I-90

I-69

Fort Wayne

Findlay

I-75

IN

Mansfield

I-71

I-71

I-90

Cleveland

Akron

I-80

I-76

I-71

I-77

Youngstown

I-80

I-76

PA

Wheeling

I-70

I-70

Dayton

I-75

Columbus

I-70

I-71

Zanesville

US-33

Athens

US-33

West Virginia

Parkersburg

I-74

Cincinnati

Chillicothe

US-23

Portsmouth

I-77

I-79

Frankfort

I-71

I-75

Kentucky

I-64

Huntington

I-64

Lexington

I-64

I-77

I-64

50 40 30 20 10 0   50   100 Miles

Ohio

Ohio

Public Library of Cincinnati-Hamilton County, Library Square, 800 Vine St., Cincinnati, OH 45202-2071. Phone: (513) 369-6000. A very good genealogy collection, local history, and early Ohio records including the Inland Waterways Library, with original records of Ohio River boat traffic from Pittsburgh to the Falls of the Ohio (Louisville), including traffic on rivers flowing into the Ohio.

Ohio Historical Society, Archives Library, 1982 Velma Ave., Columbus, OH 43211. Phone: (614) 297-2510. Serves as the state archives for Ohio. Includes many original manuscripts, biographies, genealogies, vital records. Many genealogist believe this is the number one facility in Ohio — but the Cincinnati library also claims that honor.

State Library of Ohio, Genealogy Department, 65 S. Front St., Room 308, Columbus, OH 43215. Phone: (614) 644-7061. Good genealogy collection for Ohio and states from which people migrated into Ohio including Pennsylvania, New York, and all of New England.

Alden Library, Ohio University, Park Place, Athens, OH 45701-2978. Phone: (614) 593-2703. Excellent manuscript collection. Church records, business records, county histories, biographies, and newspapers. Like another state archives.

Western Reserve Historical Society Library, 10825 E Blvd., Cleveland, OH 44106-1788. Phone: (216) 721-5722. The Western Reserve was a large region of Ohio settled by refugees of the Revolutionary War from the State of Connecticut. Collection includes original land records, New England and Pennsylvania genealogies, biographies, histories, Bibles, and much more.

Ohio Genealogical Society Library, 73 S. Main St., Mansfield, OH 44907-1644. Phone: (419) 756-7294. The best family folder collection in the state, plus many guides to county records, biographies, genealogies, and unique indexes to records.

Dayton and Montgomery County Public Library, 215 E. 3rd St., Dayton, OH 45402-2103. Phone: (937) 227-9530. The Dayton Room has one of Ohio's best genealogy collections with books, periodicals, indexes, genealogies, biographies, and more.

Rutherford B. Hays Presidential Center Library, Spiegel Grove, 1337 Hays Ave., Fremont, OH 43420-2796. Phone: (419) 332-2081. The personal library begun by President Hays is held here. The collection is strong on Ohio history, Sandusky River and Great Lakes local history, U.S. history, Black studies, and Hays family genealogy including numerous original manuscripts, and much more.

Library of Youngstown and Mahoning County, 305 Wick Ave., Youngstown, OH 44503-1079. Phone: (330) 744-8636. Good genealogy collection including oral histories, state and county histories, biographies, and genealogies. Youngstown was a crossroads for Pennsylvania and New England people entering Ohio.

Toledo — Lucas County Public Library, 325 Michigan St., Toledo, OH 43624-1614. Phone: (419) 259-5200. Records of Great Lakes traffic into Ohio via Toledo can be found here, identifying many early Ohio settlers.

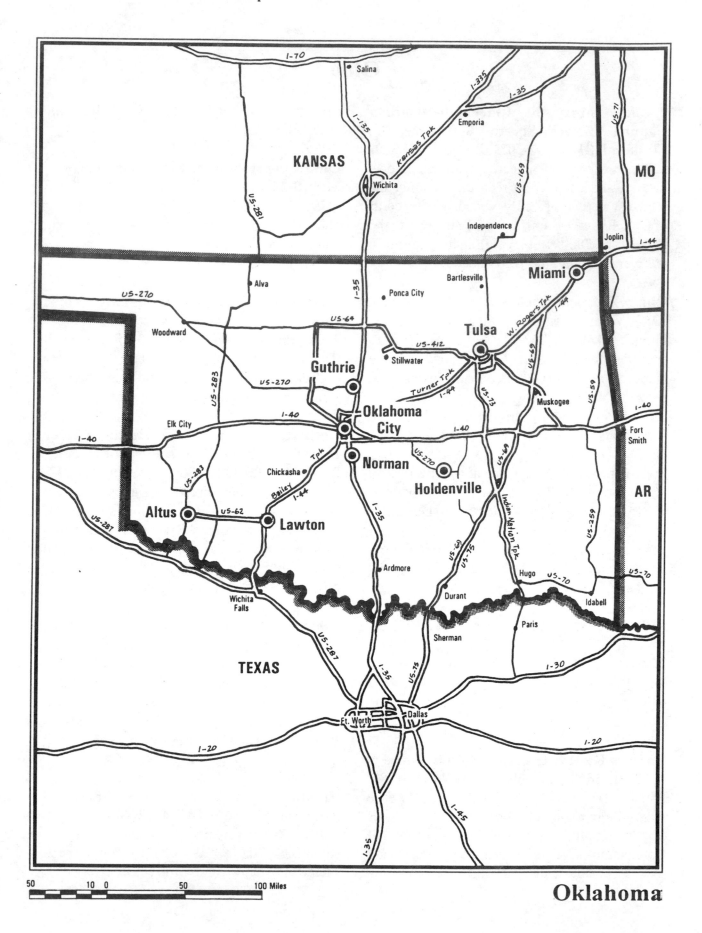

Oklahoma

Oklahoma

Oklahoma Historical Society, (Division of Library Resources/Division of Archives & Manuscripts), Wiley Post Historical Bldg., 2100 N. Lincoln Blvd., Oklahoma City, OK 73105-4997. Phone: (405) 521-2491. This facility is like two state archives: one for Native Americans, and one for the early Anglo settlers of Oklahoma. This is the starting place for Oklahoma research.

Oklahoma Department of Libraries, 200 N.E. 18th St., Oklahoma City, OK 73105-3298. Phone: (405) 521-2502. Huge book library with county histories, periodicals, indexes, reference works, maps, government publications and more.

Lawton Public Library, 110 S.W. 4th St., Lawton, OK 73501-4076. Phone: (405) 581-3450. An outstanding genealogical collection with the largest book collection of Oklahoma genealogies, plus periodicals, maps, biographies, family folders, and a statewide index to all Oklahoma Territory Tract Books (public land buyers).

Bancroft Library, University of California, Berkeley, CA 94720. Phone: (415) 642-3781. The "Bancroft Collection" is outstanding for early settlers, early trails, stagecoaches, miners, histories, etc. This library has many historical documents relating to early Oklahoma.

Bizzell Memorial Library, University of Oklahoma, 401 W. Brooks St., Norman, OK 73019. Phone: (405) 325-2611. Original historical manuscripts, county records, Spanish, Indian, military, Civil War, newspapers, cattle trails, ranching, mining, oil production, and more.

Pickens Memorial Library, 209 E. 9th St., Holdenville, OK 74848. Phone: (405) 379-3245. A very unique Native American records collection. Great records relating to the Five Civilized Tribes (and Delawares) removed to Indian Territory. This library has a surprisingly good genealogical research collection.

Oklahoma Territorial Museum Library, 406 E. Oklahoma Ave., Guthrie, OK 73044. Phone: (405) 282-1889. Territorial period of Oklahoma is well covered with many documents. Native Americans and Anglos, Intruders, Sooners, homesteaders, land rush people, and more.

Tulsa Genealogical Society Library, PO Box 585, Tulsa, OK 74101-0585. Phone: (918) 627-4224. A very large library for Oklahoma people including Bibles, cemeteries, obituaries, family folders, city directories, plat maps, and good indexes. Collection includes many references to Arkansas, Kansas, and Missouri.

Museum of the Western Prairie Library, and Western Trail Historical and Genealogical Society, 1100 Memorial Dr., PO Box 574, Altus, OK 73521-0574. Phone: (405) 482-1044. Many records for early Oklahoma settlers, obituaries, periodicals, books, histories, biographies, with many references to Texas and New Mexico people.

Miami Public Library, 200 N. Main, Miami, OK 74354. Phone: (918) 542-3064. A very good book library with emphasis on the Ozarks region of Oklahoma, Kansas, Missouri, and Arkansas. This library has a very similar collection to the Ozark Genealogical Society in Springfield, MO.

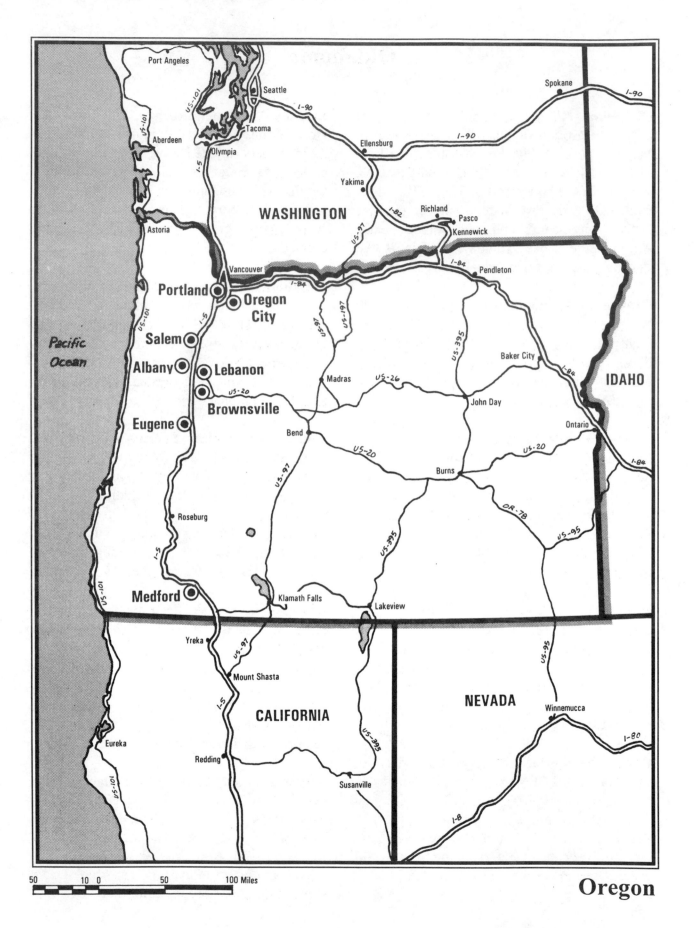

Oregon

Oregon

Oregon State Archives, 800 Summer St., N.E., Salem, OR 97310. Phone: (503) 378-0701. Naturalizations, censuses, vital records, probate records, and military records. This is the starting point for genealogical research in Oregon.

Oregon Historical Society Library, 1200 S.W. Park Ave., Portland, OR 97205. Phone: (503) 222-1741. Manuscripts, family folders, histories, biographies. Many original diaries and journals from Oregon Trail families. Excellent photograph collection of early Oregon people.

Oregon State Library, State Library Building, 250 Winter St., N.E., Salem, OR 97310. Phone: (503) 378-4243. Original county and state records including Land Donation Claims for early Oregon and Washington Territory pioneers.

Bancroft Library, University of California, Berkeley, CA 94720. Phone: (415) 642-3781. The "Bancroft Collection" is outstanding for early settlers, early trails, stagecoaches, miners, histories, etc. This library has many historical documents relating to early Oregon.

University of Oregon Library, 1299 Knight Library, Eugene, OR 97403-1299. Phone: (541) 346-3053. Enough manuscript and printed materials to qualify as Oregon's state archives.

Multnomah County Library, 205 N.E. Russell St., Portland, OR 97212-3708. Phone: (503) 248-5402. A good genealogy collection and an outstanding biographical index to early Oregon people.

Genealogical Forum of Oregon Library, 2130 S.W. 5th Ave., Suite 220, Portland, OR 97201. Phone: (503) 227-2398. A very good genealogical library with good indexes to many unique county and state records. The best surname folder collection in the state.

Linn County Historical Museum Library, 101 Park Ave., Brownsville, OR 97327. Phone: (541) 491-3978. And **Brownsville Public Library**, PO Box 68, Brownsville, OR 97327. Phone: (541) 466-5454, next door to the museum. Willamette Valley families are well covered in both facilities.

Southern Oregon Historical Society, Library Archives Department, 106 N. Central, Medford, OR 97501. Phone: (503) 773-6536. For early pioneers in Southern Oregon, this is the best place to find a reference to your ancestors.

Lebanon Public Library, 626 2nd St., Lebanon, OR 97355-3320. Phone: (541) 451-7461. Home of the *End of the Trail Research Collection* with many indexes to genealogical references, obituaries, family Bibles, early Oregon pioneers, Oregon Trail records, and more.

Oregon City Public Library, 362 Warner-Milne, Oregon City, OR 97045. Phone: (503) 657-8269. Oregon City was the end of the Oregon Trail, and the genealogical collection reflects that fact. There are many references to early Oregon settlers.

Heritage Library, 2492 Moraga, S.E., Albany, OR 97321. Phone: (541) 928-6809. A private computer database library compiled by Richard Milligan. (Open by appointment. Another contact person: Pam Knofler at (541) 928-2582). The database identifies the earliest Oregon Trail pioneers from 1846 through 1855 who came to the Oregon Country via wagon train and took Donation Land Claims.

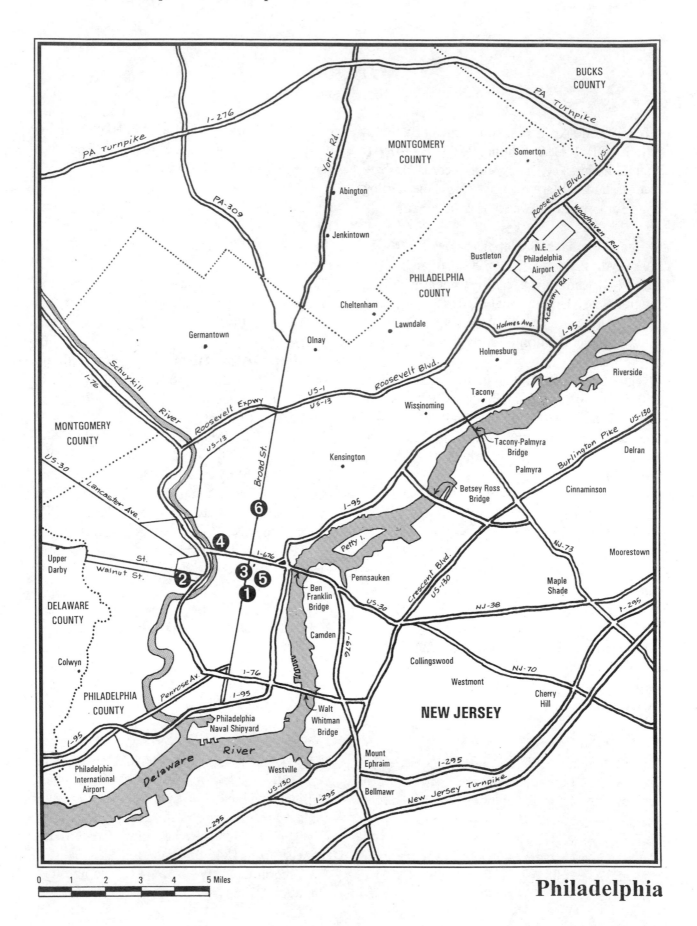

Philadelphia

Philadelphia

Note: Numbers indicate the location of each facility on the map

❶ **Historical Society of Pennsylvania Library**, 1300 Locust St., Philadelphia, PA 19107-5699. Phone: (215) 732-6200. Original records of early Quakers, Germans, Scotch-Irish, and other colonial settlers in Penn's colonies. An excellent place to locate early settlers in Pennsylvania, New Jersey, and Delaware. Many of the records have been published and are well indexed. In addition, the society has a huge manuscript collection of original documents. The society has passenger lists and indexes for the years 1800-1948 on microfilm, plus crew and vessel lists 1789-1880, and much more.

❶ **Genealogical Society of Pennsylvania**, 1305 Locust St., Philadelphia, PA 19107. Phone: (215) 545-0391. Great indexes to Pennsylvania sources. Books, periodicals, family folders, genealogies, biographies, and many research aids for Pennsylvania, and good coverage of surrounding states.

❶ **Library Company of Philadelphia**, 1314 Locust St., Philadelphia, PA 19107. Phone: (215) 546-3181. German-American collection is huge. This is also a place for locating Civil War people from Pennsylvania and early Philadelphia historical documents. This is like another city archives for Philadelphia.

❷ **Van Pelt - Dietrich Library Center**, University of Pennsylvania, 3420 Walnut St., Philadelphia, PA 19104-6206. Phone: (215) 898-7091. Huge manuscript collection, newspapers, county records, ethnic resources, denominational sources, county histories, and much more.

❸ **Philadelphia Historical Commission**, 1401 Arch St., Suite 1301, Philadelphia, PA 19102. Phone: (215) 686-4543. This is the city archives for Philadelphia, with many indexes to a broad scope of materials relating to early Philadelphia. Tax records, prisoners, commissioners reports, poor tax records, mayor's warrants and appointments, birth, death, and marriage certificates, cemetery returns, board of health reports, streets, constables, warrants and surveys, patents, city directories, and much more.

❹ **Free Library of Philadelphia**, Logan Square, Philadelphia, PA 19103-1157. Phone: (215) 686-5322. Huge book collection, periodicals, genealogies, city directories, maps, family folders, vertical files, manuscripts, and many histories for all of Pennsylvania.

❺ **National Archives**, Mid-Atlantic Region, 9th and Market Streets, Philadelphia, PA 19107. Phone: (215) 597-3000. All microfilm for the U.S. federal censuses, 1790-1920, plus all soundex indexes and virtually all printed statewide census indexes.

❻ **Urban Archives Center**, Samuel Paley Library, Temple University, Berks and 13th Sts., Philadelphia, PA 19122. Phone: (215) 204-5750. Records of churches, fraternal groups, union and guild records, and much more. A people-oriented collection of organizations, clubs, businesses, societies, and civil divisions related to the growth of Philadelphia and the impact on the surrounding area.

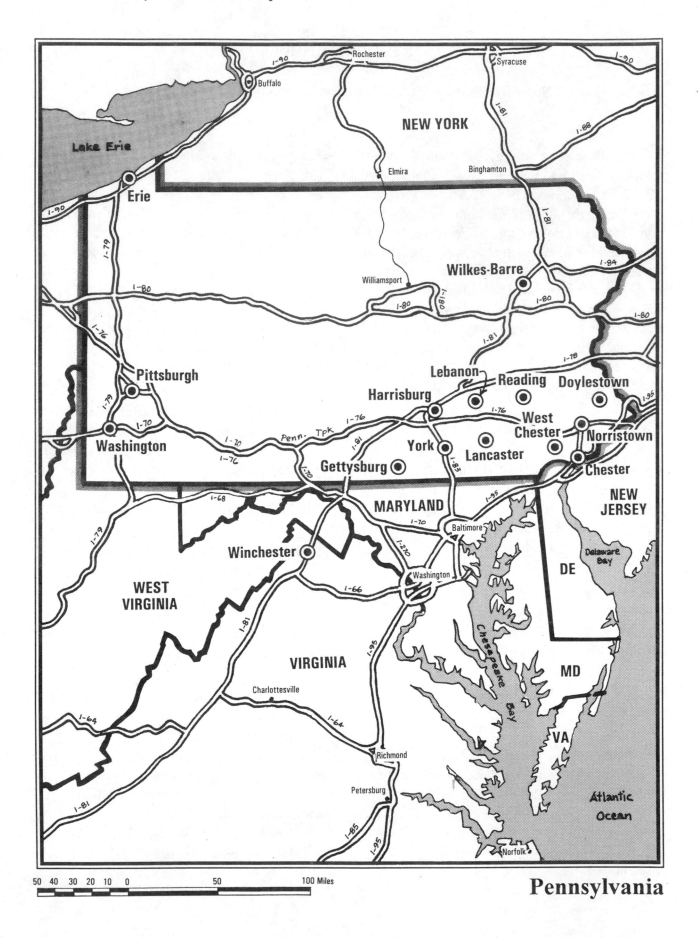

50 40 30 20 10 0   50   100 Miles

Pennsylvania

Pennsylvania (except Philadelphia)

Pennsylvania State Archives, 3rd and Forster Sts., PO Box 1026, Harrisburg, PA 17108. Phone: (717) 783-3281. The original records of the published *Pennsylvania Archives* series are here, fully indexed. It's huge!

State Library of Pennsylvania, Commonwealth Ave. and Walnut St., PO Box 1601, Harrisburg, PA 17105. Phone: (717) 787-2646. A great genealogy/local history section.

Historical Society of Western Pennsylvania, 1212 Smallman St., Pittsburgh, PA 15222. Phone: (412) 454-6000. Huge genealogical collection of the Western Pennsylvania Genealogical Society covering western Pennsylvania and eastern Ohio.

Carnegie Library of Pittsburgh, 4400 Forbes Ave., Pittsburgh, PA 15213-4080. Phone: (412) 622-3100. Huge book collection, newspapers, manuscripts, and county histories most of which have been indexed, plus family histories, family folders, local history, and genealogies.

Bishop Library, Wyoming Historical and Geological Society, 49 S. Franklin St., Wilkes-Barre, PA 18701. Phone: (717) 823-6244. An important facility for New England migrants into Pennsylvania and points south.

Handley Regional Library, 100 W. Piccadilly St., PO Box 58, Winchester, VA 22604. Phone: (540) 662-9041. A very large collection relating to the migrating Germans and Scotch-Irish who traveled the Great Valley Road from Pennsylvania to Virginia. Manuscripts, newspapers, documents, biographies, histories, and more.

Citizens Library, 55 S. College St., Washington, PA 15301. Phone: (412) 222-2400. An important portal to the Ohio River, Washington, Pennsylvania, is where many records of travelers can be found. This library has the best biographical collection of these records.

Erie County Library, 160 E. Front St., Erie, PA 16507. Phone: (814) 451-6900. The Erie Canal migrants came to Erie first, then on to Ohio and points west. This library has the best biographical collection relating to these people.

Nine county historical societies in Southeastern Pennsylvania comprise the best source for genealogical records of the early colonial immigrants to Pennsylvania:

1. **Adams County Historical Society Library**, Confederate Ave., PO Box 4325, Gettysburg, PA 17325. Phone: (717) 334-4723. **2. Bucks County Historical Society Library**, 84 Pine St., Doylestown, PA 18901. Phone: (215) 345-0210. **3. Historical Society of Berks County Library**, 940 Centre Ave., Reading, PA 19601. Phone: (610) 375-4375. **4. Chester County Historical Society Library**, 225 N. High St., West Chester, PA 19380. Phone: (610) 692-4800. **5. Delaware County Historical Society Library**, Chester, PA 19013. Phone: (610) 499-4000. **6. Lancaster County Historical Society Library**, 230 N. President Ave., Lancaster, PA 17603-3125. Phone: (717) 392-4633. **7. Lebanon County Historical Society Library**, 924 Cumberland St., Lebanon, PA 17042-5186. Phone: (717) 272-1473. **8. Historical Society of Montgomery County Library**, 1654 DeKalb St., Norristown, PA 19401. Phone: (610) 272-0297. **9. Historical Society of York County Library**, 250 E. Market St., York, PA 17403. Phone: (717) 848-1587.

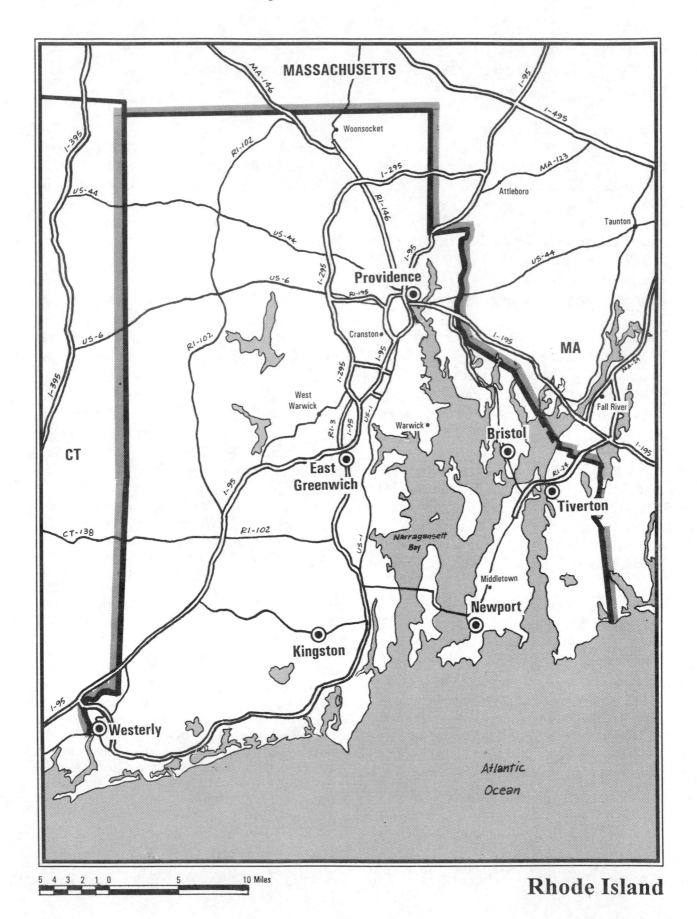

Rhode Island

Rhode Island

Rhode Island Historical Society Library, 121 Hope St., Providence, RI 02906. Phone: (401) 331-8575. The largest collection of Rhode Island genealogical materials, including original manuscripts, family Bibles, church records, histories, genealogies, family folders, and more.

Rhode Island State Library, State House, Providence, RI 02903. Phone: (401) 222-2473. Largest book library in the state with many references to Rhode Island's history. The collection includes virtually all printed histories of Rhode Island towns, biographies, genealogies, and many other records.

American Antiquarian Society Library, 185 Salisbury St., Worcester, MA 01609-1634. Phone: (508) 755-5221. Original Rhode Island town records, vital records, early newspapers, and town histories.

Rhode Island State Archives, 337 Westminster, Providence, RI 02903. Phone: (401) 222-2353. Earliest Rhode Island records to all towns and counties for colonial and federal eras. Also, same building, same phone number: **Rhode Island Records Center** with early records to Rhode Island people.

Newport Historical Society Library, 82 Touro St., Newport, RI 02840. Phone: (401) 846-0813. Largest genealogical library in the southern part of the state with a good genealogy collection relating to early Rhode Island people.

University of Rhode Island Library, 15 Lippitt Rd., Kingston, RI 02881. Phone: (401) 874-2672. Manuscripts, books, maps, biographies, histories, and more.

Roger Williams College Library, 1 Old Ferry Rd., Bristol, RI 02809. Phone: (401) 253-1040. A huge book library. Many periodicals, newspapers, biography indexes, genealogies, family histories, and the largest Baptist collection for New England.

Westerly Public Library, 44 Broad St., Westerly, RI 02891. Phone: (401) 596-2877. A large book collection for genealogy: family folders, family histories, indexes, and many references to Rhode Island families.

East Greenwich Free Library, 82 Pierce St., East Greenwich, RI 02818. Phone: (401) 884-9511. A good book collection with many genealogical references. Books, periodicals, family folders, and more.

Brown University Library, 10 Prospect St., Providence, RI 02912. Phone: (401) 863-2167. Like another state archives with a huge book library, many manuscripts relating to New England, biographies, genealogies, and more.

Davisville Free Library, Davisville Rd., North Kingston, RI 02852. Phone: (401) 884-5524. A good book collection with many genealogical references. Books, periodicals, family folders, and more.

Providence Public Library, 225 Washington St., Providence, RI 02903-3283. Phone: (401) 455-8000. A very good collection of published genealogies, biographies, periodicals, and family folders.

Tiverton Library Services, 238 Highland Rd., Tiverton, RI 02878. Phone: (401) 625-6796. A very good collection of published genealogies.

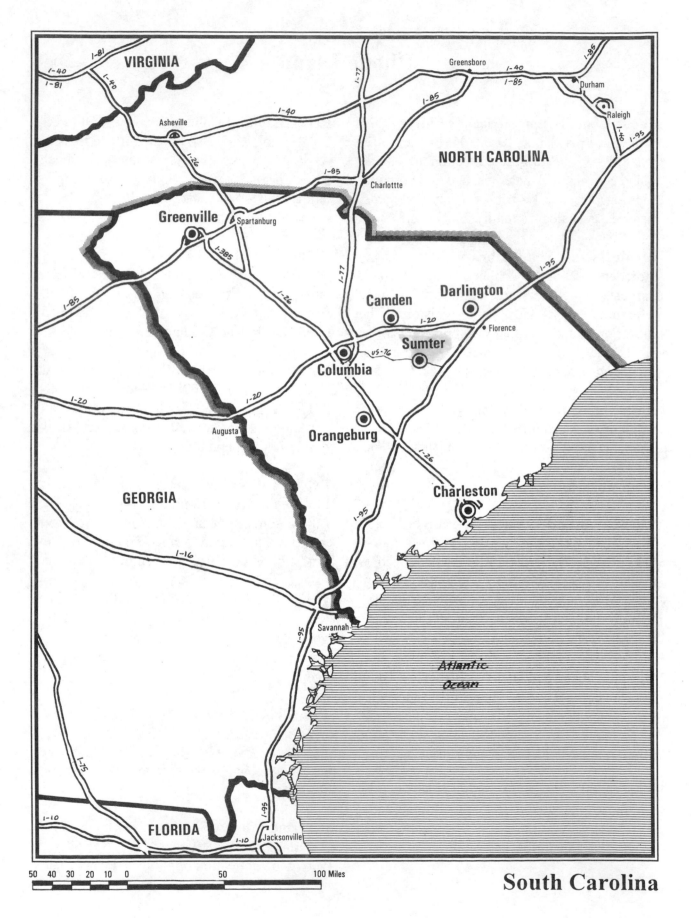

South Carolina

South Carolina

No!

South Carolina Department of Archives and History, 1430 Senate St., Capitol Station, PO Box 11669, Columbia, SC 29211-1669. Phone: (803) 734-8577. Colonial records, original county records, and best manuscript collection for the state. This facility is the best place to start for South Carolina genealogical research.

No!

South Carolina State Library, 1500 Senate St. PO Box 11469, Columbia, SC 29211. Phone: (803) 734-8666. Largest book collection in the state. Newspapers, biographies, reference works.

Sumter County Genealogical Society Library, 219 West Liberty St., Sumter, SC 29150. Phone: (803) 773-9144. This is a premier genealogical collection for all of South Carolina. The Janie Revill Collection is outstanding and well indexed. References to virtually all early South Carolina families can be found here.

No!

South Caroliniana Library, University of South Carolina, Columbia, SC 29208. Phone: (803) 777-3131. An outstanding collection for South Carolina and the South, including manuscripts, genealogies, histories, atlases, gazetteers, and more.

← 6 →

South Carolina Historical Society Library, 100 Meeting St., Charleston, SC 29401-2299. Phone: (803) 723-3225. Colonial immigrant records, biographies, genealogies, early newspapers, and more.

renovation

Brayton Collection, Santa Cruz Public Library, 224 Church St., Santa Cruz, CA 95060-3873. Phone: (408) 429-3533. Genealogical equivalent to the Draper Collection, but bigger, and with a better index. Collection is mostly compiled genealogies of early North Carolina, South Carolina, Kentucky, Tennessee, and Virginia families.

← 6 → renovation

Charleston Library Society, 164 King St., Charleston, SC 29401. Phone: (803) 723-9912. One of the finest genealogical research facilities in the South. A very large collection of family folders, genealogies, and more.

Chattanooga-Hamilton County Bicentennial Library, 1001 Broad St., Chattanooga, TN 37402-2652. Phone: (423) 757-5310. The largest family folder file collection in the Upper South, and heavy on South Carolina families.

Camden Archives and Museum Library, 1314 Broad St., Camden, SC 29020. Phone: (803) 425-6050. Another statewide collection with many indexes, bibliographies, books, periodicals, and more.

Greenville County Library, 300 College St., Greenville, SC 29601. Phone: (864) 242-5000. An excellent book library with an outstanding genealogy collection: family folders, biographies, histories, genealogies, and many references to South Carolina people.

Orangeburg County Historical Society Library, Bull and Middleton Sts., PO Box 1881, Orangeburg, SC 29116-1881. Court records, family records, deeds and mortgages, family folder files, church records, cemetery records, and many books and documents of genealogy of local families.

Darlington County Historical Commission, 204 Hewitt St., Darlington, SC 29532. Phone: (803) 398-4710. Statewide genealogy reference materials with good indexes.

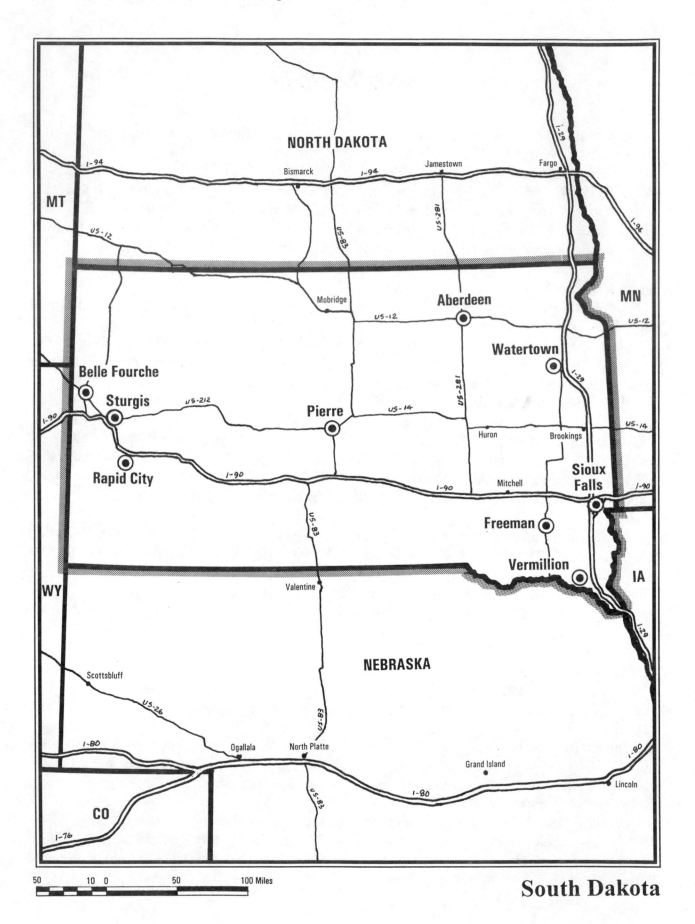

NORTH DAKOTA

I-94

Bismarck   I-94   Jamestown   Fargo   I-29

MT

US-12

I-94

US-83   US-281   MN

Mobridge   **Aberdeen**   US-12

Belle Fourche   US-12

Watertown

Belle Fourche   US-281-50   I-29

Sturgis   US-212   **Pierre**   US-14

Huron   Brookings

Rapid City   I-90   US-14

I-90   Mitchell   **Sioux Falls**   I-90

Freeman

I-90

Vermillion   IA

WY   Valentine

NEBRASKA

Scottsbluff

US-26

I-80   Ogallala   North Platte   I-80

Grand Island   Lincoln

US-83

CO

I-76   US-83   I-80

50   10 0   50   100 Miles

South Dakota

South Dakota

South Dakota State Historical Society, State Archives, 900 Governors Dr., Pierre, SD 57501-2217.Phone: (605) 773-3458. Original records for old Dakota Territory including histories, biographies, homesteads, farming, and genealogies. South Dakota's best facility.

South Dakota State Library, 800 Governors Dr., Pierre, SD 57501. Phone: (605) 773-3131. Largest book library in the state. County histories, biographies, genealogies, and more.

Rapid City Public Library, 610 Quincy St., Rapid City, SD 57701.Phone: (605) 394-4171. The South Dakota Collection is outstanding. Newspapers, obituaries, family folders, books, periodicals, biographies, and genealogies. A very good collection for research in South Dakota families

Weeks Library, 414 E. Clark St., University of South Dakota, Vermillion, SD 57069-2390. Phone: (605) 677-5371. Manuscripts, government documents, business, church, ethnic, Indians, county school archives, and more.

Alexander Mitchell Library, Aberdeen Public Library, 519 S. Kline St., Aberdeen, SD 57401-4495. Phone: (605) 626-7097. South Dakota history, genealogy, Germans from Russia, and more.

Watertown Regional Library, 611 B Ave., N.E., PO Box 250, Watertown, SD 57201-0250.Phone: (605) 882-6220. Good genealogy collection with books, periodicals, biographies, and county histories.

Belle Fourche Public Library, 905 5th Ave., Belle Fourche, SD 57717-1795. Phone: (605) 892-4407. A good genealogy library with references to early mining industries, settlers, books, and historical references.

Minnesota History Center, Historical Society of Minnesota, 45 Kellogg Blvd., W., St. Paul, MN 55102-1906. Phone: (612) 296-6980. Great genealogy collection, histories, biographies, and newspapers. The indexes to the collection include many references to South Dakota people, plus many ethnic groups that peopled South Dakota, such as the Swedes, Norwegian, Danes, and Germans.

Mikkelsen Library, Augustana College, 2001 S. Summit Ave., Sioux Falls, SD 57197-0001. Phone: (605) 336-4921. A good genealogy library. County histories, biographies, ethnic resources, and more.

Sioux Falls Public Library, 201 N. Main Ave., Sioux Falls, SD 57102-0386. Phone: (605) 367-7082. A very nice genealogy collection. Good indexes, and family folders.

Sturgis Public Library, 1040 2nd St., Sturgis, SD 57785-1595. Phone: (605) 347-2624. A small library, but with a very good genealogy collection for South Dakota.

Freeman Public Library, 185 E. 3rd St., Box I, Freeman, SD 57029. Phone: (605) 925-7003. A very good genealogy collection for South Dakota people.

National Archives, Central Plains Region, 2312 E. Bannister Rd., Kansas City, MO 64131.All microfilm for federal censuses, 1790-1920, soundex indexes, and all printed statewide census indexes. Many historical records from federal courts in South Dakota.

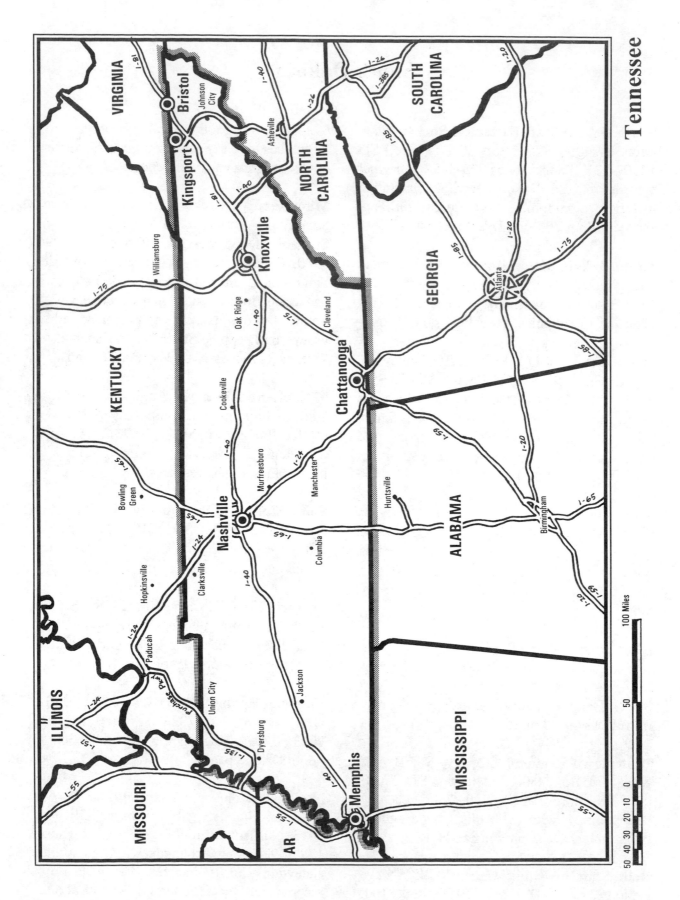

Tennessee

Tennessee

Tennessee State Library and Archives, 403 7th Ave., N., Nashville, TN 37243-0312. Phone: (615) 741-2451. Genealogy collection is outstanding. Public records, original county records, genealogies, biographies, and records of Confederate Soldiers. This is clearly the best genealogical research facility in Tennessee.

Chattanooga-Hamilton County Bicentennial Library, 1001 Broad St., Chattanooga, TN 37402-2652. Phone: (423) 757-5310. The largest family folder file collection in the Upper South, heavy on early Tennessee, North Carolina, and South Carolina families.

McClung Collection, Knox Public Library, 500 W. Church St., Knoxville, TN 37902-2505. Phone: (423) 544-5750. This historical collection for the Old Southwest includes an index to Tennessee families. There is nothing comparable to this index anywhere else in Tennessee. This library has one of the best genealogical collections in the south.

Brayton Collection, Santa Cruz Public Library, 224 Church St., Santa Cruz, CA 95060-3873. Phone: (408) 429-3526. Genealogical equivalent to the Draper Collection, but bigger, and with a better index. Collection is mostly compiled genealogies of Kentucky, Tennessee, the Carolinas, and Virginia.

Hodges Library, 1015 Volunteer Blvd., University of Tennessee, Knoxville, TN 37996-1000. Phone: (423) 974-4127. Manuscripts, biographies, genealogies, county histories, federal records, church records, ethnic, Native Americans, (especially Cherokees), river traffic, and more. An outstanding collection of historical reference material.

Tennessee Genealogical Society Library, PO Box 111249, Memphis, TN 38111-1249. Phone: (901) 381-1447. A good genealogical reference library. Many family folders, references materials, books, periodicals, county histories, and more.

Tennessee Historical Society, Ground Floor, War Memorial Building, Nashville, TN 37243. Phone: (615) 741-8934. Very good genealogy archives and library. Many indexes, cemeteries, obituaries, and more.

Kingsport Public Library, 400 Broad St., Kingsport, TN 37660-4292. Phone: (423) 229-9465. One of the largest family folder collections in the South, particularly for East Tennessee, plus a very good genealogical reference library.

Memphis-Shelby County Public Library, 1850 Peabody Ave., Memphis, TN 38104-4025. Phone: (901) 725-8855. Huge library with many books, indexes, guides and helps, periodicals, maps, biographies, family folders, county histories, and excellent statewide coverage.

Bristol Public Library, 701 Goode St., Bristol, VA 24201-4199. Phone: (540) 645-8780. Smaller family folder collection, but outstanding source for locating people coming down the Great Valley Road of Virginia and on to Tennessee and Kentucky.

Clayton Library, Center for Genealogical Research, branch of Houston Public Library, 5300 Caroline, Houston, TX 77004. Phone: (713) 284-1999. After Texas records, the premier subject in this library is Tennessee genealogical sources.

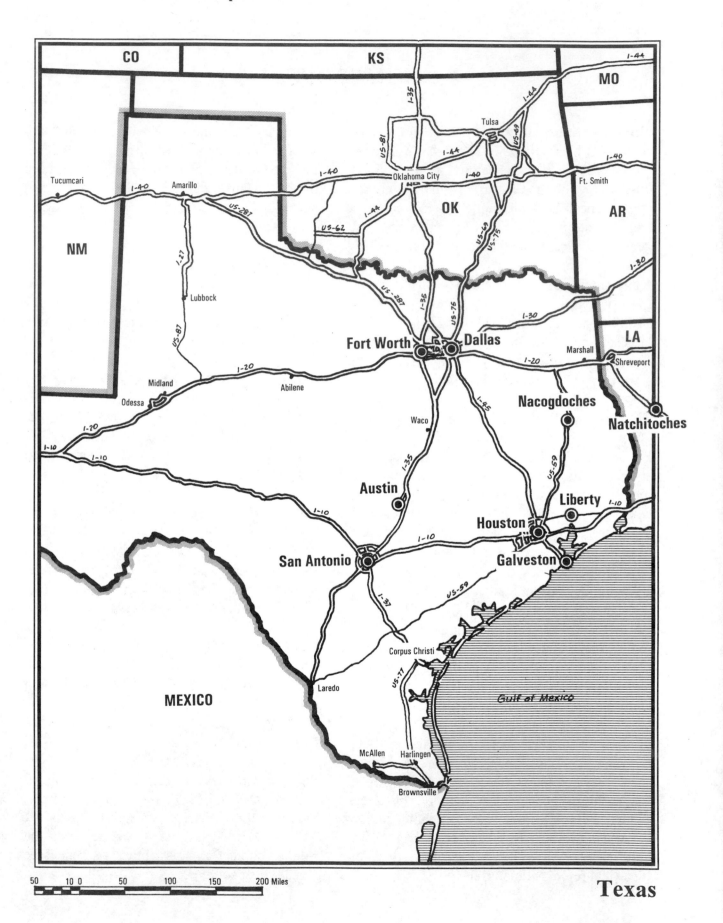

Texas

Texas

Texas State Library and Archives, 1201 Brazos, PO Box 12927, Austin, TX 78711. Phone: (512) 463-5460. Original manuscripts for Mexican Texas, Republic of Texas, and Texas State. All counties represented with original records. All Texas vital records, newspapers, books, maps, and more. One of the best genealogical collections in America.

Barker Texas History Center, UT Center for American History, SRH 2-101, Collections Deposit Library, University of Texas, Austin, TX 78712. Phone: (512) 495-4515. Historical collection is as large as the state archives. Newspapers, biographies, private collections, and more. Includes the *Natchez Trace Collection* of Mississippi, Louisiana, and Texas pioneers.

Clayton Library, Center for Genealogical Research, (branch of Houston Public Library), 5300 Caroline, Houston, TX 77004. Phone: (713) 284-1999. One of America's best places to do genealogical research, a beautiful facility just for genealogists and an outstanding collection. Genealogical references for Texas are very complete; but in addition, the library has many references to adjoining states, and is particularly strong on Tennessee resources.

Dallas Public Library, 1515 Young St., Dallas, TX 75201-9987. Phone: (214) 670-1400. An outstanding genealogical collection, with records for more than Texas including New England, Mid Atlantic, and the South.

Daughters of the Republic of Texas Library, PO Box 1401, San Antonio, TX 78295-1401. Phone: (210) 225-1071. Specializes in the colonial Mexican Texas era, and has resources from the Republic of Texas with a good collection of genealogical reference material.

San Antonio Public Library, 600 Solidad Plaza, San Antonio, TX 78205. Phone: (210) 207-4924. Excellent genealogy collection and Texana materials.

Steen Library, Steven F. Austin State University, 1936 N St., SFA Box 13055, Nacogdoches, TX 75962. Phone: (409) 468-4106. Good genealogy collection, pre-Civil War, East Texas lumber industry, oral histories, and more.

Rosenberg Library, 2310 Sealy Ave., Galveston, TX 77550-2296. Phone: (409) 763-8854. Specializes in Germans to Texas with a computer database for the Gulf Coast immigrants.

Fort Worth Public Library, 300 Taylor St., Fort Worth, TX 76102-7309. Phone: (817) 871-7740. A very good genealogical collection. Newspapers, obituaries, biographies, histories, and genealogies with good coverage for the entire Southwest.

Sam Houston Regional Library, FM 1011 Governors Rd., PO Box 310, Liberty, TX 77575-0310. Phone: (409) 336-8821. Records of the earliest settlers in Texas can be found here.

Natchitoches Genealogical and Historical Association, 2nd Floor, Parish Courthouse, PO Box 1349, Natchitoches, LA 71458-1349. Phone: (318) 357-2235. The "French Archives" has records dating back to the early 1700's, with an index kept by the Parish Court Clerk. The collection contains numerous references to Americans migrating into Texas from the 1820's, early French records, and more.

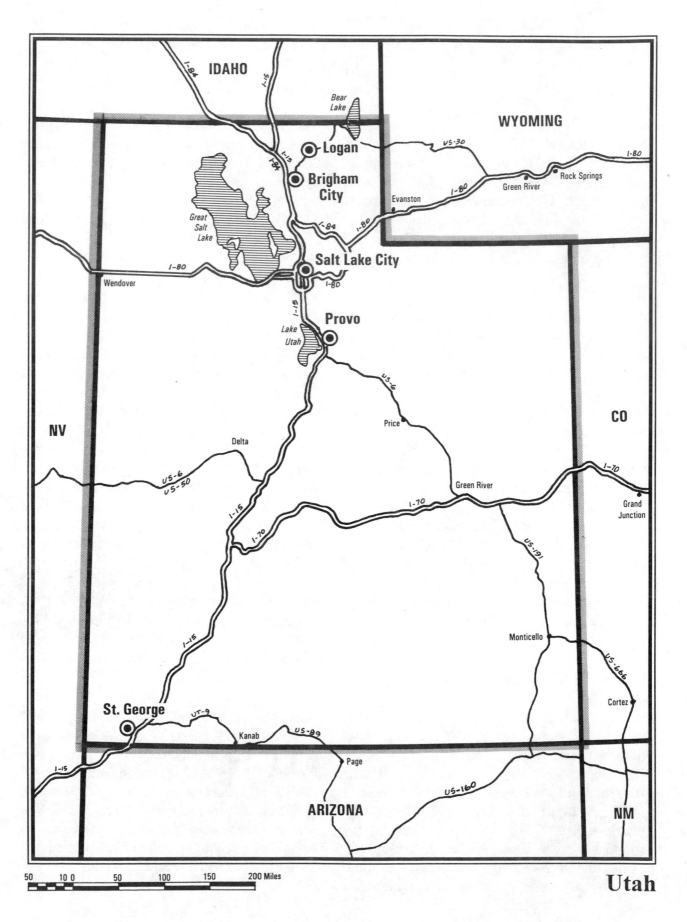

Utah

Utah

Historical Department, The Church of Jesus Christ of Latter-day Saints, Church Office Building, 50 E. North Temple, Salt lake City, UT. 84150. Phone: (801) 240-2785. This is the place — for locating records of any person who joined the Mormon Church. For early Utah people, this facility has more to offer than the Family History Library.

Pioneer Memorial Museum, Daughters of Utah Pioneers, 300 N. Main, Salt Lake City, UT 84103. Phone: (801) 538-1050. This facility has many of the records the Utah pioneers brought with them: Bibles, photographs, family journals, diaries, letters, and compiled genealogies for virtually every pioneer family who came to Utah before 1869.

Family History Library of The Church of Jesus Christ of Latter-day Saints, 35 N. West Temple St., Salt Lake City, UT 84150. Phone: (801) 240-2331. The largest genealogical library in the world. With over two million rolls of microfilm, the collection contains information from county courthouses for virtually all U.S. counties, plus an excellent array of materials from Canada, England, Wales, Scotland, Ireland, Germany, and Scandinavian countries. Every serious genealogist will make a trip to Salt Lake City sooner or later. (See page 1).

Bancroft Library, University of California, Berkeley, CA 94720. Phone: (415) 642-3781. The "Bancroft Collection" is outstanding for early settlers, early trails, stagecoaches, miners, histories, etc. This library has many historical documents relating to early Utah.

Lee Library, Brigham Young University, Provo, UT 84602. Phone: (801) 378-2905. Largest Family History Center outside Salt Lake City, but not known as well because of the dominance of the Salt Lake library. This is an excellent genealogical research library with materials relating to all states and many countries.

Utah State Historical Society, 300 Rio Grande, Salt Lake City, UT 84101-1182. Phone: (801) 533-3500. Pioneer records include mining, early settlements, colonizations, Mormons, and many records not found anywhere else relating to Utah.

Cache Valley Library, (Family History Center), 50 North Main, Logan, UT 84322. Phone: (435) 755-5594. This library has a unique collection relating to early Utah, Idaho, and Wyoming. Ranching, early settlers, cattlemen, farmers, trails, and railroading.

Everton Genealogical Library, 3223 S. Main St., Nibley, UT 84321. Phone: (435) 752-6022. How to build a library: first, publish the largest magazine in the country for genealogists, *The Genealogical Helper*, second, accept books for review in the magazine, and third, place all submitted books in your own library. Following that plan since 1947, Everton's library has gathered over 36,000 books related to genealogy, many of which can be found nowhere else. The collection includes many obscure family histories (many of which were self-published in small quantities). This library is worth a visit by genealogists en route to Salt Lake City.

Val A. Browning Library, Dixie College, 225 S. 700 E., St. George, UT 84770. Phone: (435) 652-7714. A very large manuscript collection on early Utah pioneers, and a large genealogy collection, including many records from out-of-state.

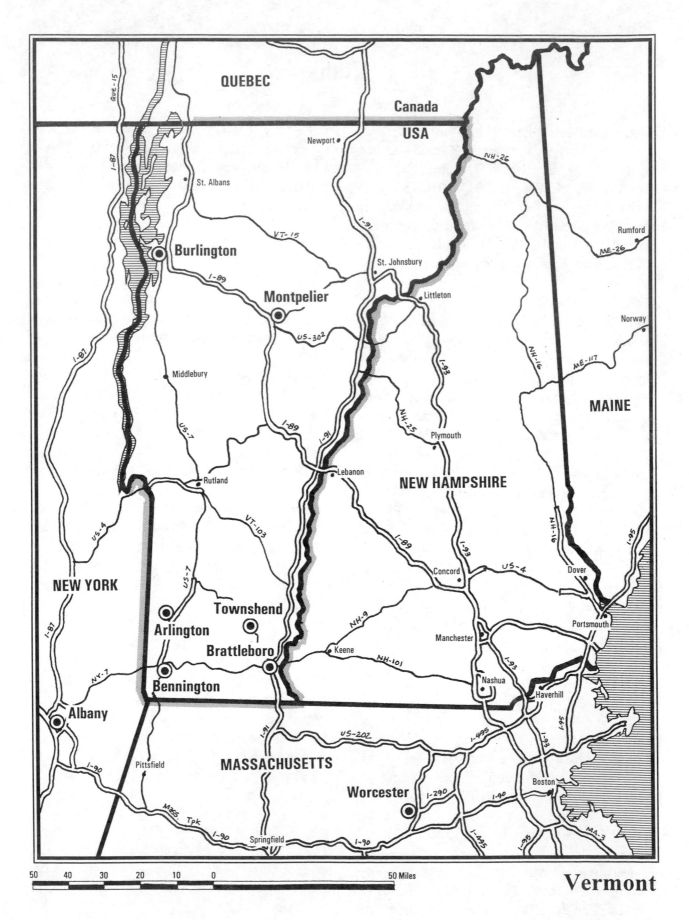

Vermont

General Services Center - Reference Research Section, Drawer 33, Montpelier, VT 05633-7601. Phone: (802) 828-3286. This is the Vermont State Historical Society and is clearly the best research center for locating early Vermont people with many manuscripts, family histories, periodicals, maps, and many family folders.

Vermont State Archives, 26 Terrace St., Montpelier, Vermont. Mail: 109 State St., Montpelier, VT 05609-1103. Phone: (802) 828-2369. Original state, county, and town records are well covered for the entire state including records from all levels of government.

American Antiquarian Society Library, 185 Salisbury St., Worcester, MA 01609-1634. Phone: (508) 755-5221 This library is known for its outstanding newspaper collection including many from Vermont. In addition, Vermont historical references are numerous.

Genealogy/History Library, Bennington Museum, W. Main St., Bennington, VT 05201. Phone: (802) 447-1571. Early Connecticut, New York, and Vermont records.

Bailey-Howe Memorial Library, University of Vermont, Burlington, VT 05405-0036. Phone: (802) 656-2020. Vermont local histories, oral histories, Civil War, and more.

Albany Institute of History and Art, McKinney Library, 125 Washington Ave., Albany, NY 12210-2296. Phone: (518) 463-4478. The facility has the best indexes to the original records from the early 1600's including references to families moving into Old Albany county during the colonial period (Albany County once included all of Upper New York

and all of Vermont).

Brattleboro Historical Society Library, PO Box 6392, Brattleboro, VT 05301. Phone: (802) 254-5037. A good regional library with many genealogies, family folders, books, periodicals, maps, indexes to records, cemeteries, obituaries, and more.

Vermont State Library, State Office Building, 109 State St., Montpelier VT 05602. Phone: (802) 828-3261. Large book library, with many periodicals and a great historical reference collection.

Vermont Old Cemetery Association, PO Box 132, Townshend, VT 05353. The best statewide cemetery records for all of Vermont, with great indexes to burials in virtually all cemeteries in the state.

Brooks Memorial Library, 224 Main St., Brattleboro, VT 05301. Phone: (802) 254-5290. A very large genealogical collection with books, periodicals, family folders, genealogies, newspapers, obituaries, biographies, and many indexes to the genealogical records.

Russell Vermontiana Collection of Martha Canfield Library, Main St., Arlington, VT 05250. Phone: (802) 375-6309. Many rare books and unique genealogical sources to early Vermont people. Call for an appointment.

Columbia County Historical Society Library, 5 Albany Ave., PO Box 311, Kinderhook, NY 12106. Phone: (518) 758-9265. Located on the Hudson River and the main migration route across New England to interior New York, this library has a huge collection of family folders for early people, including many from Vermont.

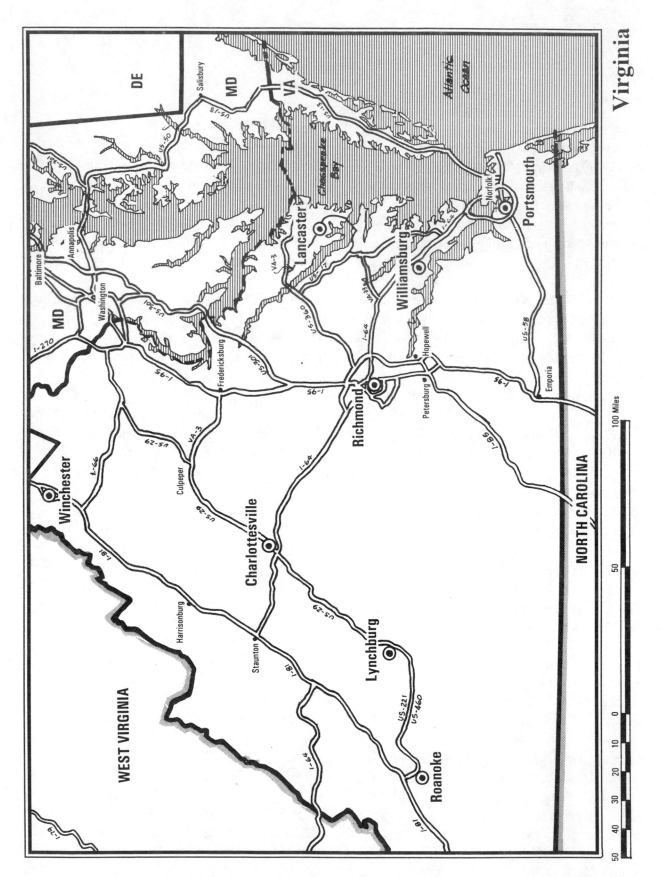

Virginia

Virginia

Virginia Historical Society Library, 428 North Blvd., PO Box 7311, Richmond, VA 23221-0311. Phone: (804) 358-4901. Original county records, militia lists, bounty lands, tax lists, poll lists, genealogies, newspapers, and family Bibles. This facility has 900 index drawers indexing 10 million documents relating to the Old Dominion, including Virginia, West Virginia, and Kentucky.

Library of Virginia, Virginia State Library and Archives, 800 E. Broad St., Richmond, VA 23219-1905. Phone: (804) 692-3500. A very large genealogical collection including family Bible records, vital records, histories, biographies, and newspapers. Many of the scanned manuscripts of this library are now available on the Internet, along with a facsimile card catalog index to its holdings.

Mary Ball Washington Museum and Library, Route 3, Old Jail Bldg., Old Clerks Office Bldg., and Lancaster House, PO Box 97, Lancaster, VA 22503-0097. Phone: (804) 462-7280. A name index resides in this little library taken from virtually every history book published on Virginia and Kentucky including biographies, county histories, community and town histories, militia records, and fraternal organization records.

Swem Library, College of William and Mary, PO Box 8794, Williamsburg, VA 23187-8794. Phone: (757) 221-4636. The famous "Swem Index" to Virginia settlers, plus original records from the Jamestown settlement, Virginia Company, manuscripts, journals, and much more. This is the library for primary research for the earliest Virginia colonists, dating from 1607. The genealogical references are numerous.

Alderman Library, University of Virginia, Charlottesville, VA 22903-2498. Phone: (804) 924-3026. Like another state archives for Virginia. A large genealogical collection, colonial records, federal, private, state, and original manuscripts.

Handley Regional Library, 100 W. Piccadilly St., PO Box 58, Winchester, VA 22604. Phone: (540) 662-9041. A very large collection relating to the migrating Germans and Scotch-Irish who traveled the Great Valley Road of Virginia. Manuscripts, newspapers, documents, biographies, histories, and more.

Brayton Collection, Santa Cruz Public Library, 224 Church St., Santa Cruz, CA 95060-3873. Phone: (408) 429-3532. Genealogical equivalent to the Draper Collection, but larger, and with a better index. The collection has many compiled genealogies of Virginia families.

Roanoke County Public Library, 3131 Electric Rd. S.W., Roanoke, VA 24018-6496. Phone: (540) 772-7507. A great library for southwest Virginia with many family folders, books, genealogies, and indexes to records.

Jones Memorial Library, 2311 Memorial Ave., Lynchburg, VA 24501. Phone: (804) 846-0501. An excellent collection of historical materials, family folders, and genealogies relating to people coming from the tideland region, crossing the Blue Ridge Mountains, and on to the Great Valley of Virginia. Many of these people came through Lynchburg.

Portsmouth Public Library, 601 Court St., Portsmouth, VA 23704. Phone: (757) 393-8501. A very good genealogical collection.

John D. Rockefeller, Jr. Library
313 First St
Colonial Williamsburg Foundation, Williamsburg Va 23815-1776

(757) 565-8511
Juleigh Muirhead Clark
Public Services Librarian

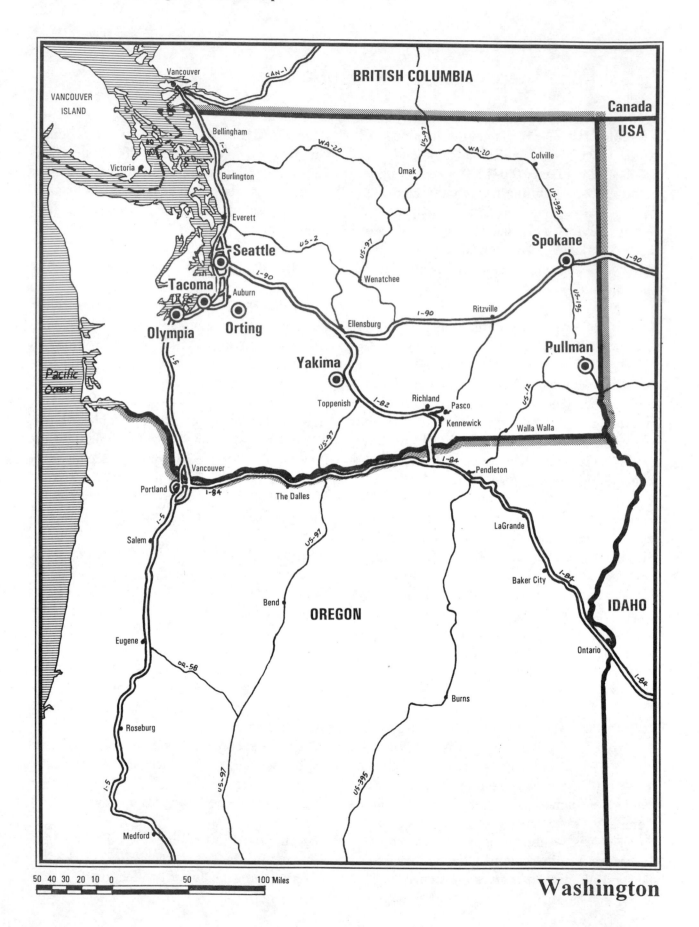

Washington

Washington

Seattle Public Library, Genealogy Department, 1000 4th Ave., Seattle, WA 98104. Phone: (206) 386-4100. One must visit Seattle to discover that this library rivals any other genealogical library on the west coast in size and quality. Outside of Seattle, it is not well known, but it features an outstanding genealogy collection, including many federal censuses on microfilm, family folders, and very good coverage for the entire U.S. for published vitals, records for all states, periodicals, county histories, and many family histories. In addition, the library has a comprehensive biographical index to Washington settlers, pioneers, and notables, and houses a very large newspaper collection.

Washington State Archives, 1120 Washington St., S.E., (EA-11), Olympia, WA 98504. Phone: (360) 753-5485. A good collection of reference materials with genealogical value.

Washington State Historical Society, Research Library, 315 N. Stadium Way, Tacoma, WA 98406. Phone: (253) 798-5914. Like another state archives.

Washington State Library, Genealogy Department, Capitol Campus, PO Box 42460, Olympia, WA. 98504-2460. Phone: (360) 753-4024. Very good genealogy collection.

Suzzallo Library, University of Washington, Seattle, WA 98195-0001. Phone: (206) 543-0242. The Pacific Northwest and Alaska coverage for historical materials is outstanding.

Holland Library, Washington State University, Pullman, WA 99164-5610. Phone: (509) 335-4557. The best collection for Eastern Washington settlers, original manuscripts, and histories. Many genealogical resources can be found.

Seattle Genealogical Society Library, 8511 15th Ave. N.E., PO Box 75388, Seattle, WA 98125-0388. Phone: (206) 522-8658. Largest family folder collection in the state, plus many books, periodicals, genealogies, biographies, and histories.

Tacoma Public Library, 1102 Tacoma Ave. S., Tacoma, WA 98402-2098. Phone: (253) 591-5622. Good genealogy collection, state births and deaths on microfilm, periodicals, genealogies, and biographical records.

Heritage Quest Research Library, 220 W. Bridge St., PO Box 1119, Orting, WA 98360. Phone: (360) 893-2799. A private membership library featuring census films, books, periodicals, genealogies, biographies, county histories, and many computer indexes. The collection has many out-of-state references, plus many foreign countries are represented.

Eastern Washington State Historical Society Library, 2316 W. 1st Ave., Spokane, WA 99204-1099. Phone: (509) 456-3931. Very good genealogical collection, including county and local histories, biographies, migrations, cattlemen, settlers, and family folders. Coverage is for Washington, Oregon, Idaho, and Montana.

Yakima Valley Genealogical Society Library, 221 East B St., PO Box 445, Yakima, WA 98907. Phone: (509) 248-1328. A very active genealogical group, and a very good genealogy library with many historical references. The Yakima Valley region is represented with many family folders, unpublished genealogies, and biographies.

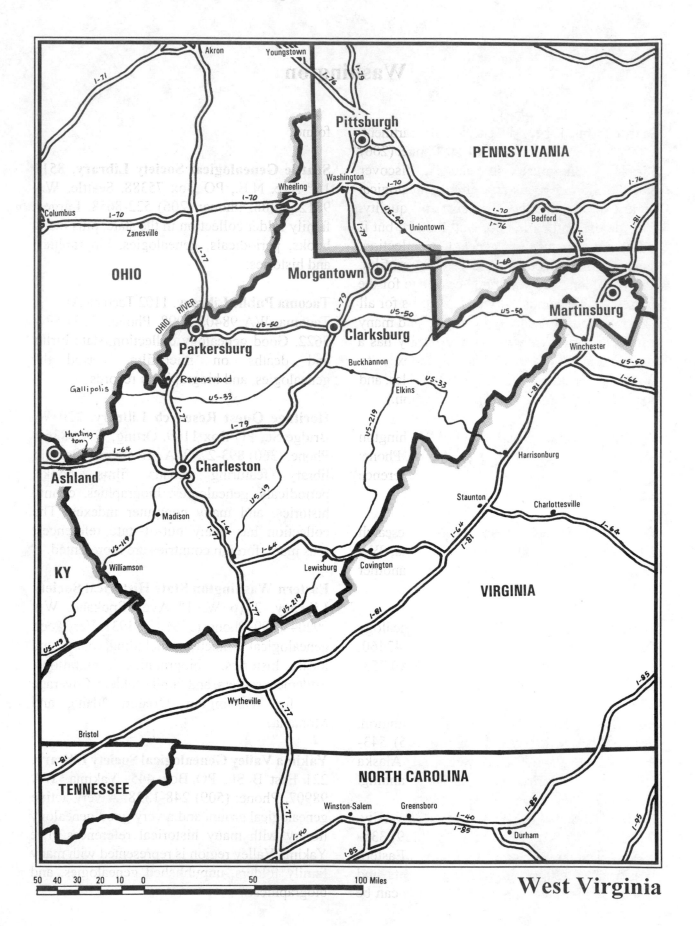

West Virginia

West Virginia

West Virginia Archives and History Division Library, Cultural Center, 1900 Kanawha Blvd., E., Charleston, WV 25305. Phone: (304) 558-0230. Original manuscripts, biographies, county histories, tax records, and more. This is the starting place for West Virginia research.

Virginia Historical Society Library, 428 North Blvd., PO Box 7311, Richmond, VA 23221-0311. Phone: (804) 358-4901.Original county records, militia lists, bounty lands, tax lists, poll lists, genealogies, newspapers, and family Bibles. This facility has 900 index drawers indexing 10 million documents, including the area of Virginia that became West Virginia. There may be more resources about early West Virginia in this facility than exists anywhere in West Virginia.

Mary Ball Washington Museum and Library, Route 3, Old Jail Bldg., Old Clerks Office Bldg., and Lancaster House, PO Box 97, Lancaster, VA 22503-0097. Phone: (804) 462-7280. A name index resides in this little library taken from virtually every history book published on Virginia, West Virginia, and Kentucky.

West Virginia and Regional History Collection, Colson Hall, West Virginia University Libraries, PO Box 6464, Morgantown, WV 26506. Phone: (304) 293-3536. Largest manuscript collection in the state.

University of Chicago Library, 1100 E. 57th St., Chicago, IL 60637-1502. Phone: (773) 702-4085. Home of *The Durrett Collection* which contains historical manuscripts relating to Kentucky, West Virginia, and the Ohio River Valley, comparable to the Draper Collection.

Parkersburg-Wood County Public Library, 3100 Emerson Ave., Parkersburg, WV 26101. Phone: (304) 420-45887. The collection of the West Augusta Historical and Genealogical Society contains genealogies, family histories, cemetery records, obituaries, and many family folders. Coverage is for the northwestern part of West Virginia, and parts of Southwest Pennsylvania.

Clarksburg-Harrison Public Library, 404 W. Pike St., Clarksburg, WV 26301. Phone: (304) 624-6512. Large genealogical library with many indexes, periodicals, histories, obituaries, cemeteries, family folders, and more.

Historical Society of Western Pennsylvania, 1212 Smallman St., Pittsburgh, PA 15222. Phone: (412) 454-6000. Colonial records of the Ohio Company with land grants and references to the original settlements in Southwestern Pennsylvania and Old Northwestern Virginia (the area which became West Virginia). Records dating from the 1750's can be found in this library.

Martinsburg-Berkeley County Public Library, 101 W. King St., Martinsburg, WV 25401. Phone: (304) 267-8933. Very good genealogy collection with many historic references to earliest settlers of West Virginia.

Boyd County Public Library, 1740 Central Ave., Ashland, KY 41101. Phone: (606) 329-0090. Located near the juncture of Ohio, Kentucky, and West Virginia, this library has collected many genealogical references to West Virginia people, including family folders, biographies, genealogies, and more. Strong on early Virginia pedigrees.

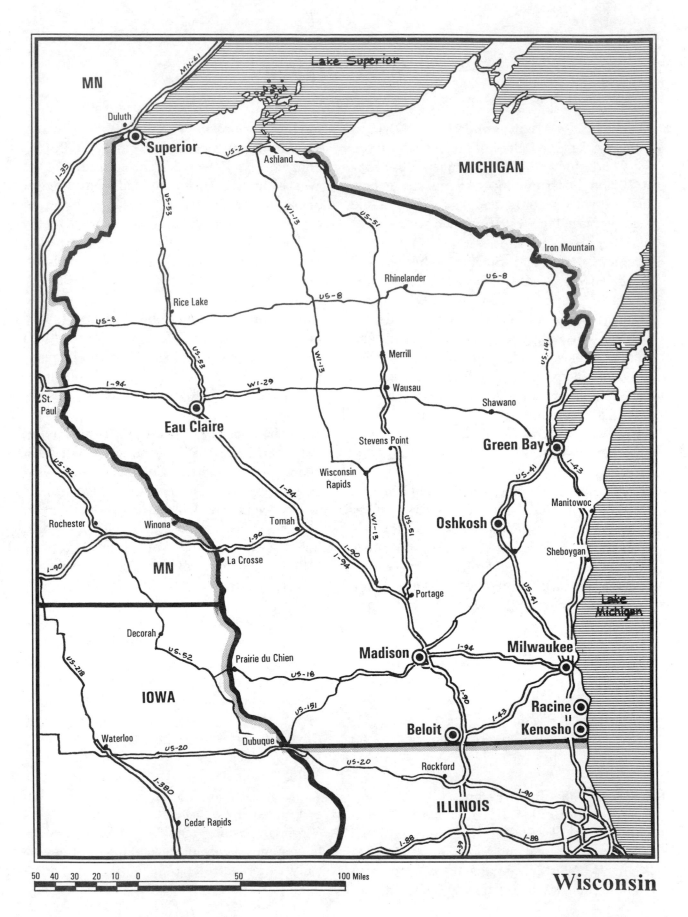

Lake Superior

MN

Duluth

Superior

Ashland

MICHIGAN

MN-61

US-2

US-53

WI-13

US-51

Iron Mountain

Rhinelander

US-8

I-35

Rice Lake

US-8

US-8

Merrill

US-53

WI-13

US-51

St. Paul

I-94

WI-29

Wausau

Shawano

Eau Claire

Stevens Point

Green Bay

I-43

US-52

Wisconsin Rapids

Manitowoc

Rochester

Winona

Tomah

WI-13

US-51

Oshkosh

Sheboygan

I-90

I-90

La Crosse

MN

I-94

US-41

Portage

Lake Michigan

Decorah

US-52

Prairie du Chien

Madison

I-94

Milwaukee

US-218

US-18

IOWA

US-151

I-90

I-43

Racine

Waterloo

US-20

Dubuque

Beloit

Kenosho

I-380

Rockford

US-20

Cedar Rapids

I-88

ILLINOIS

I-88

I-39

I-90

50 40 30 20 10 0   50   100 Miles

Wisconsin

Wisconsin

State Historical Society of Wisconsin Library, 816 State St., Madison, WI 53706. Phone: (608) 264-6400. The best manuscript collection in the state, plus censuses, tax records, land records, and much more. This library holds the famed "Draper Papers", a large collection of interviews, genealogies, and histories of early pioneers compiled by Lyman Draper, former head of the Library. Most of the Draper Papers record the lives of settlers of the Appalachian regions of Western Virginia, Kentucky, Tennessee, North Carolina, and South Carolina. The society library also has the holdings of the Wisconsin State Old Cemetery Society, identifying burials in the earliest cemeteries in the state.

Milwaukee Public Library, 814 W. Wisconsin Ave., Milwaukee, WI 53233-2385. Phone: (414) 286-3020. A very large genealogy collection with family folders, biographies, statewide aids, indexes, obituaries, newspapers, and much information about the German immigrants to Wisconsin.

Golda Meir Library, University of Wisconsin - Milwaukee, 2311 E. Hartford Ave., PO Box 604, Milwaukee, WI 53201. Phone: (414) 229-4785. A great historical collection, particularly for German immigrants, and one of America's best map collections.

Oshkosh Public Library, 106 Washington Ave., Oshkosh, WI 54901-4985. Phone: (920) 236-5200. Books, periodicals, family folders, indexes, and more.

Milwaukee County Historical Society, 910 N. Old World 3rd St., Milwaukee, WI 53203. Phone: (414)

273-8288. Huge manuscript collection, many books, periodicals, and surname folders with a strong emphasis on German immigrant families.

Beloit Public Library, 409 Pleasant St., Beloit, WI 53511-6279. Phone: (608) 364-2905. A good genealogical collection with many books, periodicals, family folders, and more.

McIntyre Library, University of Wisconsin - Eau Claire, 105 Garfield Ave., Eau Claire, WI 54702-4004. Phone: (715) 836-3715. Large manuscript and book collection with many historical references.

Brown County Library, 515 Pine St., Green Bay, WI 54301. Phone: (920) 983-0955. A very large genealogy section, with an excellent array of general genealogical materials, plus local histories, county histories, newspapers, obituaries, family folders, and more.

Memorial Library, University of Wisconsin - Madison, 728 State St., Madison, WI 53706. Phone: (608) 262-3193. A very large manuscript collection with many historical references.

Kenosho Public Library, 711 59th Pl., Kenosho, WI 53140. Phone: (414) 942-3700. Good genealogy collection.

Racine County Historical Society, Archive of County History and Genealogy, 701 Main St., Racine, WI 53401-1527. Phone: (414) 639-2069. Very good genealogy collection.

Superior Public Library, 1530 Tower Ave., Superior, WI 54880. Phone: (715) 394-0248. Very good genealogy collection.

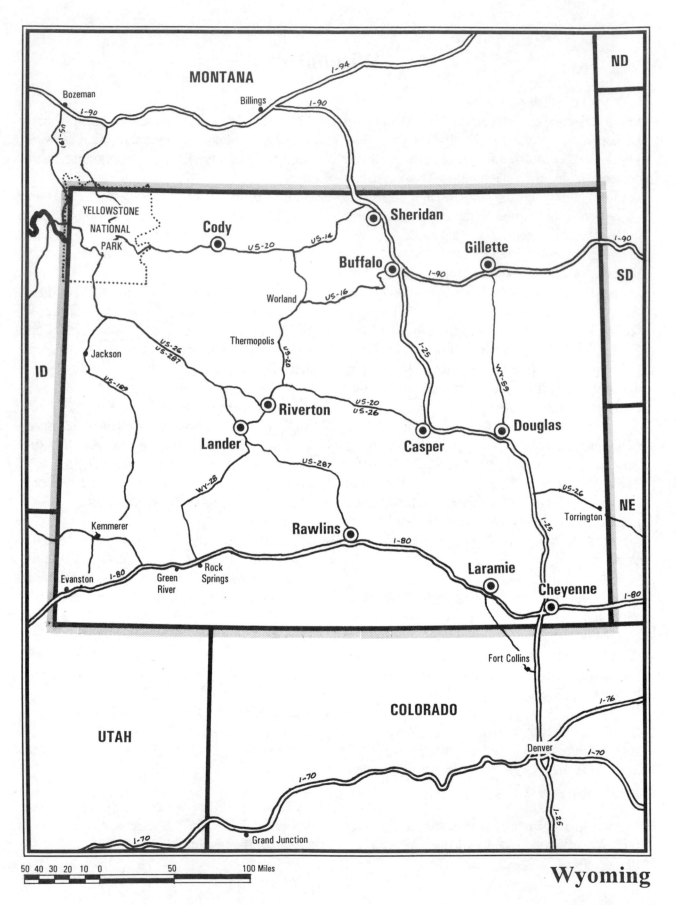

Wyoming

Wyoming

Wyoming State Archives Museum and Historical Department, Barrett Building, 24th and Central, Cheyenne, WY 82002. Phone: (307) 777-7519. The best manuscript collection in the state. This is the place to start for Wyoming genealogy.

Wyoming State Historical Society, Barrett Building, 24th and Central, Cheyenne, WY 82002. Phone: (307) 777-7014. Newspapers, biographies, genealogies, county histories, cattlemen, cattle drives, homesteaders, and more.

Wyoming State Library, Supreme Court and Library Building, Cheyenne, WY 82002. Phone: (307) 777-7281. Large book library and good genealogy collection.

University of Wyoming Library, University Station, PO Box 3334, Laramie, WY 82071-3334. Phone: (307) 766-3279. Excellent book collection, plus a huge manuscript collection, periodicals, and more. Excellent collection of Wyoming history, genealogy, cattle ranches, and pioneers.

Laramie County Library, 2800 Central Ave., Cheyenne, WY 82001-2799. Phone: (307) 634-3561. Largest book collection for genealogy in the state, plus family folders, government documents, and many references to Wyoming homesteading, pioneers, cattlemen, farmers and more.

Johnson County Library, 171 N. Adams, Buffalo, WY 82834. Phone: (307) 684-5546. A very good genealogy library with many biographies, genealogies, and indexes.

Natrona County Public Library, 307 E. 2nd Ave., Casper, WY 82601-2598. Phone: (307) 237-4935. A good-sized genealogy library, supported by local genealogists.

Park County Library, 1057 Sheridan Ave., Cody, WY 82414. Phone: (307) 587-6204. A good genealogy collection for all of Wyoming.

Campbell County Public Library, 2101 4J Rd., Gillette, WY 82718. Phone: (307) 682-3223. The facility serves a large region of Wyoming, with a good genealogical society supporting the genealogical collection at the library.

Carbon County Public Library, Carbon Building, W. Buffalo and 3rd St., Rawlins, WY 82301. Phone: (307) 328-2618. A good genealogy collection.

Fulmer Library, 335 W. Alger St., Sheridan, WY 82801-3899. Phone: (307) 674-8585. This library has a very good genealogy collection including a large oral history project. The local genealogical society is very active and supports the library with volunteers.

Fremont County Library, 451 N. 2nd St., Lander, WY 82520. Phone: (307) 332-5194. A good genealogy collection for all of Wyoming.

Riverton Public Library, 1330 W. Park Ave., Riverton, WY 82501-3249. Phone: (307) 856-3556. Very good genealogy collection.

Converse County Library, 300 Walnut, Douglas, WY 82633. Phone: (307) 358-3644.

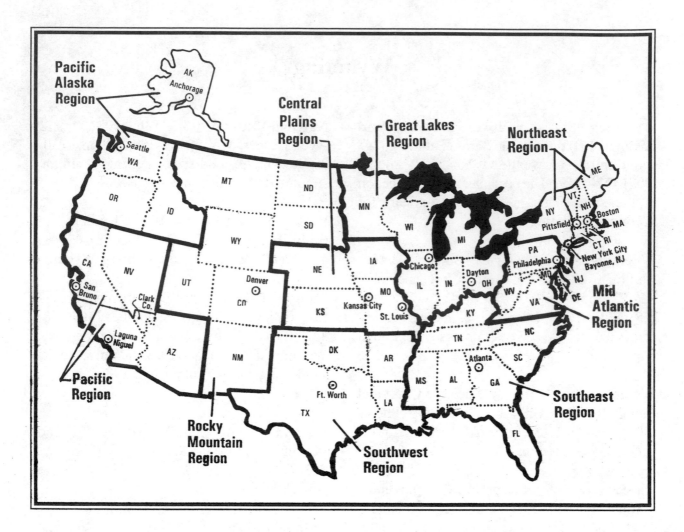

National Archives Regions and Facilities

Northeast Region
- Boston (Waltham), Massachusetts
- Pittsfield, Massachusetts
- New York City, New York
- Bayonne, New Jersey

Mid Atlantic Region
- Center City Philadelphia, Pennsylvania
- Northeast Philadelphia, Pennsylvania

Southeast Region
- Atlanta (East Point), Georgia

Great Lakes Region
- Chicago, Illinois
- Dayton, Ohio

Central Plains Region
- Kansas City, Missouri

Southwest Region
- Fort Worth, Texas

Rocky Mountain Region
- Denver, Colorado

Pacific Region
- Laguna Niguel, California
- San Francisco (San Bruno), California

Pacific Alaska Region
- Seattle, Washington
- Anchorage, Alaska

National Personnel Records Center
- **Military Records Facility**
  St. Louis, MO
- **Civilian Records Facility**
  St. Louis, MO

National Archives

Regional Facilities

Regional Records Services Facilities of the National Archives and Records Administration hold significant archival and microfilm collections. Well used by genealogists, each regional facility holds federal records for a number of states; and most of the facilities hold a complete set of microfilm for all federal censuses, military records; and ship passenger lists for various ports of the U.S.

Less known to genealogists, these regional archives are where a researcher may find a reference to an ancestor's court case in a U.S. territorial court, federal district court, federal circuit court, or a Confederate states district court. All cases for the federal circuit courts (1789-1912) and the federal district courts (1789 - 1939) are indexed by the name of the plaintiff as well as the defendant in the *Federal Digest*. (The *Federal Digest* can be found in many law libraries in the U.S.). The original court case files for early federal court cases can be found today in the National Archives Records Services Facility covering the state in which the federal court was located.

Before accessing the records in these regional facilities, a researcher should consult the *Guide to Federal Records in the National Archives of the United States*, (Washington, DC: National Archives, 1995, 3 vols.), which identifies the record groups and the nature of the records held in Washington, DC, College Park, MD, and all of the regional facilities of the National Archives. A copy of this valuable 3-volume guide can be found in all National Archives reading rooms. Researchers should also consult *Genealogical Research in the National Archives* (Washington, DC: National Archives Trust Fund Board, 1982) to determine the nature of records having genealogical value held by the National Archives.

For each of the Regional Records Services Facilities, a description of their holdings is shown, as follows on the next page.

Northeast Region

♦ ♦ ♦ ♦

Boston, MA

Address: Northeast Region, National Archives and Records Administration, Frederick C. Murphy Federal Center, 380 Trapelo Road, Waltham, MA 02154-6399.

Phone: (781) 647-8104
Fax: (781) 647-8088.
E-mail:center@waltham.nara.gov

Region of coverage: Connecticut, Maine, Massachusetts, New Hampshire, Rhode Island, and Vermont.

General: The archives has more than 25,000 cubic feet of archival holdings dating from 1789 to the 1970's including primarily textual documents, but also some photographs, maps, and architectural drawings. These records were created by over 80 Federal agencies in the Northeast Region.

Archival Holdings: Among subjects of local interest are: War of 1812 prize cases in Massachusetts; fortifications, lighthouses, life saving stations, and other coastal facilities; the Passamaquoddy Tidal Power Project in Maine during the 1930's; World War II era research projects at Harvard University and the Massachusetts Institute of Technology; and federal court, naval, Coast Guard, and customs activities. Records available to researchers also include court records from federal, U.S. district, and bankruptcy courts in the six New England states, and from the First Circuit Court of Appeals, Boston.

Microfilm Holdings: The Boston facility has extensive holdings of National Archives microfilm publications for the study of history, economics, public administration, political science, law, westward expansion, scientific exploration, ethnology, genealogy, and other subjects. Included are records of the Continental Congress, the Supreme Court of the United States, material relating to the Revolutionary and Civil Wars, German records captured at the end of World War II, and territorial papers.

Genealogical Holdings: Records include federal population censuses for all states, 1790-1920 (including indexes for 1880, 1900, 1910, and 1920); Revolutionary War military service records; pension and bounty land warrant applications; passenger arrival records for the port of Boston, 1820-74, 1883-1930, and for other New England ports since 1900; Canadian border entry records, 1894-1954; and records relating to appointments of certain federal officials.

Pittsfield, MA

Address: Northeast Region, National Archives and Records Administration, 100 Dan Fox Drive, Pittsfield, MA 01201-8230.

Phone: (413) 445-6885
Fax: (413) 445-7305
E-mail: center@pittsfield.nara.gov

Region of coverage: Connecticut, Maine, Massachusetts, New Hampshire, New York, Rhode Island, and Vermont.

General: NARA's Northeast Region (Pittsfield) has almost 60,000 rolls of National Archives microfilm publications, many of special interest to genealogy researchers, created to allow access to information while preserving original documents from deterioration and damage from handling.

Census Records: Microfilm copies of the existing federal population census schedules taken every ten years, for all states from 1790 to 1920 (nearly all 1890 schedules were destroyed by fire in 1921). The facility also has Soundex indexes to the 1880, 1900, and 1920 censuses and a partial Soundex index (for 21 States) to the 1910 census.

Military Records: Microfilm copies of the military service records of Revolutionary War soldiers and pension and bounty land warrants issued to veterans of that war. These records cover all States and include name indexes. In addition, there are indexes to compiled military service records of volunteer soldiers who served between 1784 and 1901; a register of enlistments for the U.S. Army, 1798-1914; records of the 54th Massachusetts Volunteer Infantry, 1863-1865 (the Glory Regiment); indexes to pension records for veterans of the Mexican War, 1892- 1926; and World War I Selective Service draft registration cards, 1917 - 1918, for Connecticut, Maine, Massachusetts, New Hampshire, New York, and Rhode Island.

Naturalization Records: Microfilm holdings include an index to New England naturalization petitions, 1791-1906; an index to naturalization petitions and records of the U.S. District Court, 1906-1966, and the U.S. Circuit Court, 1906-1911, for the District of Massachusetts; and petitions and other naturalization records of the U.S. District Court and Circuit Courts of the District of Massachusetts, 1906-1929.

Passenger Arrival Records: Microfilm copies of ship manifests of passengers into the ports of Boston (1820-1943), New York (1820-1957),

and Philadelphia (1800-1882). Records of miscellaneous Atlantic and Gulf ports are available as are manifests of passengers arriving in the St. Albans, Vermont, District through Canadian Pacific and Atlantic ports, 1895-1954. Records for other smaller ports, such as New Bedford, Massachusetts, Providence, Rhode Island, and Portland, Maine, are also available.

Other Records of Interest: Three microfilm publications useful for genealogical research on Native Americans are: Eastern Cherokee Applications of the U.S. Court of Claims, 1906-1909 (M1104); Enrollment Cards for the Five Civilized Tribes, 1898-1914 (M1186); and Final Rolls of Citizens and Freedmen of the Five Civilized Tribes (T529). In addition, microfilm is available for the Air Force's Project Bluebook; appointments of postmasters, 1832-1950, Post Office reports of site locations, 1837-1950; and Russian consulates in the United States, 1861-1922.

New York City

Address: Northeast Region, National Archives and Records Administration, 201 Varick Street, New York, NY 10014-4811.

Phone: (212) 337-1300.
Fax: (212) 337-1306.
E-mail: archives@newyork.nara.gov

Region of Coverage: New Jersey, New York, Puerto Rico, and the U.S. Virgin Islands.

General: This regional archives has more than 63,000 cubic feet of archival holdings dating from 1685 to the 1980's including textual documents, photographs, maps, and architectural drawings. These archival holdings were created or received by the federal courts and over 60 federal agencies in the Northeast

Region. Federal law requires that agencies transfer permanently valuable, noncurrent records to NARA. Subjects covered include early politics, the evolution of federal courts, Constitutional rights, sectional conflict, the Civil War, immigration through Castle Garden and Ellis Island, Chinese exclusion, economic development, business, organized crime, invention, the arts, censorship, World Wars I and II, the New Deal, and the Cold War. Historic names in the files include Alexander Hamilton, Aaron Burr, Samuel Colt, Susan B. Anthony, Charles Goodyear, Alexander Graham Bell, Thomas Alva Edison, the Lusitania, the Titanic, Emma Goldman, Marcus Garvey, Adam Clayton Powell, Dutch Schultz, Jimmy Hoffa, the Rosenbergs, and Alger Hiss.

Microfilm Holdings: The New York City facility has extensive holdings of National Archives microfilm publications for the study of history, economics, public administration, political science, law, ethnology, genealogy, and other subjects. Included are records of U.S. diplomatic missions, material relating to the Revolutionary and Civil Wars, German records captured at the end of World War II, and territorial papers.

Genealogical Holdings: Records include federal population censuses for all states, 1790-1920 (including indexes for 1880, 1900, 1910, and 1920); military service records, pension and bounty land warrant applications; passenger lists of vessels arriving at New York; naturalization indexes for New York and New Jersey; and World War II concentration camp records.

Bayonne, NJ

Address: Northeast Region, National Archives and Records Administration, Building 22,

Military Ocean Terminal, Bayonne, New Jersey 07002-5388.

Phone: (201) 823-7241
Fax: (201) 823-5432
E-mail: center@bayonne.nara.gov

Region of coverage: New Jersey, New York, Puerto Rico, and the U.S. Virgin Islands.

General: This facility is primarily a records management center in which federal agencies deposit records for a period of time prior to destruction.

Public Records Holdings: While most records center holdings are not open to the public except through the agencies that created or received them, there are some important exceptions, including closed corporate and personal bankruptcy case files from the U.S. Bankruptcy Courts and civil and criminal cases from the U.S. District Courts in the Northeast Region.

Mid-Atlantic Region

◆ ◆ ◆ ◆

Center City Philadelphia

Address: Mid Atlantic Region, National Archives and Records Administration, 9th and Market Sts, Philadelphia, PA 19107-4292.

Phone: (215) 597-3000
Fax: (215) 597-2303
E-mail: archives@philarch.nara.gov

Region of coverage: Delaware, Maryland, Pennsylvania, Virginia, and West Virginia.

General: NARA's Mid Atlantic Region (Center City Philadelphia) has more than 40,000 cubic feet of archival holdings including textual documents, photographs, maps, and architectural drawings, dating from 1789 to 1989. These archival holdings were created or received by the federal courts and over 50 federal agencies in the Mid-Atlantic region.

Archival Holdings: Subjects covered include Chinese-Americans, the home-front during World War II, National Park Service sites, service in the merchant marine, violations of federal laws such as tax evasion and smuggling, and the work of U.S. Army Corps of Engineers.

Genealogical Holdings: The Center City Philadelphia facility has extensive holdings of National Archives microfilm publications. Chief among them for genealogical research are federal population censuses for all states, 1790-1920 (including indexes for 1880, 1900, 1910, and 1920). Other microfilm publications of genealogical interest include military service records, passenger arrival lists from Philadelphia and Baltimore, pension and bounty land warrant applications, and federal court records including naturalizations. The facility also has microfilm publications related to pre-federal and early federal history, U.S. diplomacy, the land and other natural resources, military history and other subjects. A catalog of Microfilm Publications in the National Archives-Mid Atlantic Region is available upon request.

Northeast Philadelphia

Address: Northeast Region, National Archives and Records Administration, 14700 Townsend Road, Philadelphia, PA 19154-1096.

Phone: (215) 671-9027
Fax: (215) 671-0273
E-mail: center@philfrc.nara.gov

Region of coverage: Delaware, Pennsylvania, Maryland, Virginia, and West Virginia.

General: This facility is primarily a records management center in which federal agencies deposit records for a period of time prior to destruction.

Public Records Holdings: While most records holdings are not open to the public except through the agencies that created or received them, there are some important exceptions including closed corporate and personal bankruptcy case files from the U.S. Bankruptcy Courts and civil and criminal cases from the U.S. District Courts in the Northeast Region.

Southeast Region

✦ ✦ ✦ ✦

Atlanta, GA

Address: Southwest Region, National Archives and Records Administration, 1557 St. Joseph Ave., East Point, Georgia 30344-2593.

Phone: (404) 763-7477.
Fax: (404) 763-7033.
E-Mail: center@atlanta.nara.gov

Region of coverage: Alabama, Florida, Georgia, Kentucky, Mississippi, North Carolina, South Carolina, and Tennessee.

Archival Holdings: This regional archives has about 70,000 cubic feet of archival holdings dating from 1716 to the 1980's, primarily textual records but also maps, photographs, and architectural drawings. These records were created or received by the federal courts and over 100 federal agencies, and are unique evidence of the impact of Federal Government policies and programs in the southeast region. Federal law requires that agencies transfer permanently valuable, noncurrent records to NARA. Among the subjects included are: the Vice Admiralty Court of the Province of South Carolina, the evolution of federal courts, Constitutional rights, the Civil War and reconstruction, economic development, business, organized crime, invention, the arts, censorship, World Wars I and II, the New Deal, and space exploration. Historic names in the files include Wernher Von Braun, Andrew Johnson, David Lilienthal, Martin Luther King, Jr., and Andrew Young.

Microfilm Holdings: The Atlanta facility has extensive holdings of microfilm publications, which include basic documentation for the study of history, economics, public administration, political science, law, ethnology, genealogy, and other subjects. Included are records of U.S. diplomatic missions, material relating to the Revolutionary War, the Civil War, and World War II.

Genealogical Holdings: Records include federal population censuses for all states, 1790-1920 (including indexes for 1880, 1900, 1910, and 1920); military service records and indexes; pension and bounty-land warrant applications; indexes to passengers arrival records for eastern and Gulf Coast ports; indexes to naturalization records in federal courts throughout the Southeast; and records relating to Native Americans and African Americans.

Great Lakes Region

◆ ◆ ◆ ◆

Chicago, IL

Address: Great Lakes Region, National Archives and Records Administration, 7358 S. Pulaski Rd., Chicago, IL 60629-5898.

Phone: (773) 581-7816.
Fax: (312) 886-7883.
E-mail: center@chicago.nara.gov

Region of Coverage: Illinois, Indiana, Michigan, Minnesota, Ohio, and Wisconsin.

Archival Holdings: The Great Lakes Region (Chicago) has more than 64,000 cubic feet of historical records dating from 1800 to the 1980's including textual records and nontextual records such as maps and photographs from federal courts and some 85 federal agencies in Illinois, Indiana, Michigan, Minnesota, Ohio, and Wisconsin. Federal law requires that agencies transfer permanently valuable, noncurrent records to NARA. Among subjects covered by the records are the Great Lakes and inland waterways; Native Americans; the environment; immigration and naturalization; inventions and technology; railroads; the automotive industry; the labor movement; organized crime; domestic conditions during World Wars I and II; sedition and treason; and nuclear energy research. Historic names in the records range from Aaron Burr and Abraham Lincoln to Marcus Garvey and Al Capone. Historical themes documented range from the early nineteenth century opening of Midwestern public lands to the development of space exploration technology. Records available to the public include court records from federal, U.S. district and Bankruptcy

Courts in Illinois, Indiana, Michigan, Minnesota, Ohio, and Wisconsin. Information about access to court case files stored at the Chicago facility is available online.

Microfilm Holdings: The Chicago facility has extensive holdings of microfilm publications for the study of history, economics, public administration, political science, law, ethnology, genealogy, and other subjects. Included are records on U.S. diplomatic missions, Native American affairs, the Revolutionary and Civil Wars, and German documents captured at the end of World War II.

Genealogical Holdings: Records include federal population censuses for all states, 1790-1920; some military service and pension records, and bounty land warrant applications; selected passenger arrival records and indexes for vessels arriving at New York and other U.S. ports; a naturalization index covering parts of Illinois, Indiana, Iowa, and Wisconsin; and Indian census rolls for Michigan, Minnesota, and Wisconsin.

Dayton, OH

Address: Great Lakes Region (Dayton), National Archives and Records Administration, 3150 Springboro Rd., Dayton, OH 45439-1883

Phone: (937) 225-2852
Fax: (937) 225-7236
E-mail: center@dayton.nara.gov

Region of covrage: Ohio

General: This facility is primarily a records management center in which federal agencies deposit records for a period of time prior to destruction.

Public Records Holdings: While most records holdings are not open to the public except through the agencies that created or received them, there are some important exceptions, including closed corporate and personal bankruptcy case files from the U.S. Bankruptcy Courts and civil and criminal cases from the U.S. District Courts in Ohio.

Central Plains Region

◆ ◆ ◆ ◆

Kansas City, MO

Address: Central Plains Region, National Archives and Records Administration, 2312 East Bannister Rd., Kansas City, MO 64131-3011.

Phone: (816) 926-6920.
Fax: (816) 926-6982.
E-mail: center@kansascity.nara.gov

Region of coverage: Iowa, Kansas, Minnesota, Missouri, Nebraska, North Dakota, and South Dakota.

General: NARA's Central Plains Region in Kansas City has more than 35,000 cubic feet of archival holdings including textual documents, photographs, maps, and architectural drawings, dating from about 1821 to the 1980's. These archival holdings were created or received by the federal courts and over 70 federal agencies.

Archival Holdings: Among subjects of local interest are: frontier and territorial history;

American Indians native to the Northern Great Plains; the development of natural resources; court cases involving fugitive slave Dred Scott, Birdman of Alcatraz Robert Stroud, and automobile entrepreneur Henry Ford. Records available to the public include case files from federal, U.S. District and Bankruptcy Courts in Iowa, Kansas, Missouri, and Nebraska, and the Eighth Circuit Court of Appeals. Information about access to court case files stored at the Kansas City facility is available online.

Microfilm Holdings: The Kansas City facility has extensive holdings of National Archives microfilm publications for the study of history, economics, public administration, political science, law, ethnology, genealogy, and other subjects. Included are records of U.S. diplomatic missions, material relating to the Revolutionary and Civil Wars, German records captured at the end of World War II, and territorial papers.

Genealogical records include federal population censuses for all states, 1790-1920 (including indexes for 1880, 1900, 1910, and 1920); military service records, pension and bounty land warrant applications; censuses and land allotment files for Native Americans.

Southwest Region

Fort Worth, Texas

Address: Southwest Region, National Archives and Records Administration, 501 West Felix St., Bldg 1, PO 6216, Fort Worth, TX 76115-0216.

Phone: (817) 334-5515
Fax: (817) 334-5511
E-mail: center@ftworth.nara.gov

Region of coverage: Arkansas, Oklahoma, Louisiana, and Texas.

General: The Southwest Region in Fort Worth has more than 66,000 cubic feet of archival holdings dating from 1806 to the 1980's including textual documents, photographs, and maps. These archival holdings were created or received by the federal courts and 85 federal agencies in the southwest region.

Archival Holdings: Among the subjects covered are regional and national history from the early 1800's with emphasis on westward expansion to the Southwest and the settlement of Native Americans (particularly Cherokees, Choctaws, Chickasaws, Creeks, and Seminoles) in Indian Territory; include the Civil War, slavery, Chinese exclusion, repatriation, segregation, World Wars I and II, treason, business, economic development, oil, and the space program. Historic names and topics include Jackson Burnett, Bonnie and Clyde, the Blue Angels, the Dalton Gang, Wyatt Earp, Billie Sol Estes, Henry O. Flipper, the Green Corn Rebellion, O. Henry, Andrew Jackson, Machine Gun Kelly, Jean Lafitte, Madalynn Murray O'Hair, Isaac Parker, Belle Starr, and the Texas City disaster. Records available to the public include case files from federal, U.S. District and Bankruptcy Courts in Arkansas, Louisiana, Oklahoma, and Texas. Information on access to court case files stored at the Fort Worth facility is available online.

Microfilm Holdings: The Fort Worth facility has extensive holdings of National Archives microfilm publications for the study of history, economics, public administration, political science, law, ethnology, genealogy, and other subjects. Included are records of U.S. diplomatic missions, material relating to the Revolutionary and Civil Wars, German records captured at the end of World War II, and territorial papers.

Genealogical Holdings: Records include federal population censuses for all states, 1790-1920 (including indexes for 1880, 1900, 1910, and 1920); military service records, pension and bounty land warrant applications; passenger lists; and Dawes census cards and enrollment jackets for the Five Tribes of Oklahoma.

Rocky Mountain Region

◆ ◆ ◆ ◆

Denver, CO

Address: Rocky Mountain Region, National Archives and Records Administration, Bldg. 48, Denver Federal Center, PO Box 25307, Denver, CO 80225-0307.

Phone: (303) 236-0804.
Fax: (303) 236-9297.
E-mail: center@denver.nara.gov

Region of Coverage: Colorado, Montana, New Mexico, North Dakota, South Dakota, Utah, and Wyoming.

Archival Holdings: This regional archives has more than 35,000 cubic feet of archival holdings open to the public for research. These holdings date from about 1860 to the 1980's and include textual records, photographs, maps, and architectural drawings. They were created or received by the federal courts and over 75 federal agencies in the region covered. Among subjects of local interest are homesteading, Indian history, mining, reclamation, and the proceedings of the territorial courts.

Microfilm Holdings: The Denver facility has extensive holdings of microfilm publications.

Included are records of U.S. diplomatic missions, material relating to the Revolutionary and Civil Wars, German records captured at the end of World War II, and territorial papers.

Genealogical Holdings: Records include federal population censuses for all states, 1790 1920 (including indexes for 1880, 1900, 1910, and 1920); military service records; pension and bounty land warrant applications; Indian censuses; Utah polygamy prosecution case files; and Colorado naturalizations.

Pacific Region

◆ ◆ ◆ ◆

Laguna Niguel, CA

Address: Pacific Region, National Archives and Records Administration, 24000 Avila Road, 1st Floor, East Entrance, PO Box 6719, Laguna Niguel, CA 92607-6719.

Phone: (714) 360-2626
Fax: (714) 360-2624
E-Mail: center@laguna.nara.gov

Region of coverage: Arizona, Southern California (all counties south of and including San Luis Obispo, Kern, and San Bernardino), and Clark County, Nevada.

General: The Laguna Niguel facility has more than 28,000 cubic feet of archival holdings dating from about 1850 to the 1980's. In addition to textual records, there are architectural drawings, maps, and photographs. These holdings were created or received by the federal courts and over 50 federal agencies in the Pacific Region.

Archival Holdings: Among the subjects covered are private land claims of the Spanish and Mexican periods in California history; the opening of the public domain to homestead settlement; the impact of the railroads on Native American life and culture; ethnic diversity, Chinese exclusion, and immigration and naturalization; the maritime industry and its development; the buildup of coastal defenses and military bases since the Spanish-American War; the growth of the naval bases and their relationship to and impact on local communities; the development of Corps of Engineers civil works projects relating to flood control, beach erosion control, pollution abatement, and the uses of navigable waterways. Selected finding aids, including a comprehensive guide to the archival holdings, are available by mail and online. Research can be initiated in person, or by telephone, mail, fax, or electronic mail. Records available to the public include court records from federal, U.S. District and Bankruptcy Courts in Arizona, Southern California, and Clark County, Nevada. Information on access to court case files stored at the Laguna facility is available online.

Microfilm Holdings: The Laguna Niguel facility has extensive holdings of National Archives microfilm publications for the study of history, economics, public administration, political science, law, ethnology, genealogy, and other subjects. Included are records of U.S. diplomatic missions, material relating to the Revolutionary, Mexican, Civil, Spanish-American Wars, German records captured at the end of World War II, and territorial papers.

Genealogical Holdings: Records include federal population censuses for all states, 1790-1920 (including indexes for 1880, 1900, 1910, and 1920); censuses of Native Americans

living on reservations in Southern California and Arizona; indexes to compiled military service records; military post returns for forts in California and Arizona; and pension and bounty land warrant applications and indexes.

San Francisco

Address: Pacific Region, National Archives and Records Administration, 1000 Commodore Dr., San Bruno, CA 94066-2350.

Phone: (650) 876-9001.
Fax: (650) 876-0920.
E-mail: center@sanbruno.nara.gov

Region of coverage: Northern California (all counties north of and not including San Luis Obisbo, Kern, and San Bernardino), Guam, Hawaii, Nevada (except Clark County), American Samoa, and the Trust Territory of the Pacific Islands.

General: The San Francisco facility has more than 44,000 cubic feet of archival holdings dating from 1850 to the 1980's including textual documents, photographs, maps, and architectural drawings. These archival holdings were created or received by the federal courts and more than 100 federal agencies in the Pacific Region.

Archival Holdings: Among the subjects covered are Chinese exclusion and immigration, the development of Pearl Harbor and mainland coastal fortifications, land use, mining, migrant labor camps, and tribal claims. Records available to the public include closed corporate and personal bankruptcy case files, and civil and criminal case files from the U.S. District Courts in Northern California, Nevada (except Clark County), and Hawaii.

Information about court case files stored at the San Francisco facility are available online.

Genealogical Holdings: The San Francisco facility has extensive holdings of National Archives microfilm publications including many of genealogical interest. These include federal population censuses for all states, 1790-1920 (including indexes for 1880, 1900, 1910, and 1920); censuses listing residents of American Samoa and Native Americans in California and Nevada; maritime records for San Francisco and other ports; military service records; pension and bounty land warrant applications; and U.S. court records. The facility also has microfilm publications related to pre-federal and early federal history, the land and other natural resources, military history, and U.S. diplomacy.

Pacific Alaska Region

◆ ◆ ◆ ◆

Seattle, WA

Address: Pacific Alaska Region, National Archives and Records Administration, 6125 Sand Point Way N.E., Seattle, WA 98115-7999.

Phone: (206) 526-6501.
Fax: (206) 526-6575
E-mail: center@seattle.nara.gov

Region of coverage: Idaho, Oregon, and Washington.

General: The Seattle facility has more than 30,000 cubic feet of archival holdings, including textual documents, photographs, maps, and architectural drawings, dating from the 1850's to the 1980's. These archival holdings were created or received by the federal courts and over 60 federal agencies in Idaho, Oregon, and Washington. Federal law requires that agencies transfer permanently valuable, noncurrent records to NARA.

Archival Holdings: Among subjects of local interest are: Chinese exclusion, the home-front during World War II, the work of the U.S. Army Corps of Engineers, Native Americans, the merchant marine service, and smuggling. Records available to the public include case files from federal, U.S. district and bankruptcy courts in Idaho, Oregon, and Washington. Information on access to court case files stored at the Seattle facility is available online.

Microfilm Holdings: The Seattle facility has extensive holdings of microfilm publications for the study of history, economics, public administration, political science, law, ethnology, genealogy, and other subjects. Included are: records of U.S. diplomatic missions worldwide, material relating to the Revolutionary and Civil Wars, German records captured at the end of World War II, and territorial papers. Selected microfilm can be loaned to academic institutions.

Genealogical Holdings: Records of interest include federal population censuses for all states, 1790-1920 (including indexes for 1880, 1900, 1910, and 1920); military service records; pension and bounty land warrant applications; some passenger arrival and naturalization records; and records relating to the Five Civilized Tribes. This microfilm is not available on loan.

Anchorage, AK

Address: Pacific Alaska Region, National Archives and Records Administration, 654 W. 3rd Ave., Anchorage, AK 99501-2145.

Phone: (907) 271-2441
Fax: (907) 271-2442
E-mail: archives@alaska.nara.gov

Region of coverage: Alaska

Archival Holdings: The archives has more than 9,000 cubic feet of archival holdings including textual documents, photographs, maps, and architectural drawings, dating from about 1867 to the present. These archival holdings were created or received by the federal courts and over 30 federal agencies in Alaska. Federal law requires that agencies transfer permanently valuable, noncurrent records to NARA. Subjects covered include federal courts; land and resource management; agriculture; forestry; Native American affairs; weather observations; commercial shipping and commerce; roads, railroads, and other transportation; economic development; and military and naval activities.

Microfilm Holdings: The Anchorage facility has over 65,000 rolls of National Archives microfilm publications including territorial papers, federal government of Alaska, the Alaska Railroad, material relating to the Revolutionary and Civil Wars, German records captured at the end of World War II, and the Russian-American Company.

Genealogical Holdings: Microfilm holdings include military service records; pension and bounty land warrant applications; passenger arrival records; Indian censuses; naturalization records; and federal population censuses for all states, 1790-1920 (including indexes for 1880, 1900, 1910, and 1920).

National Personnel Records Center
Military Records Facility
St. Louis, MO

Address: National Archives and Records Administration, National Personnel Records Center (Military Records Facility), 9700 Page Ave., St. Louis, MO 63132-5100.

General: For a person who served in the military in the 20th century, it is possible to obtain limited vital and personal information from that person's military records file. If the subject person is deceased, even more vital information can be obtained, such as the date and place of birth, date and place of death, and place of last residence. A standard form SF-80 must be used to request copies from a military file. A copy of the SF-80 can be obtained from the address listed above.

National Personnel Records Center
Civilian Records Facility
St. Louis, MO

Address: National Archives and Records Administration, National Personnel Records Center (Civilian Records Facility), 111 Winnebago St., St. Louis, MO 63118-4199.

General: This facility holds personnel records of Federal Government employees whose employment ended after about 1910. Records less than 75 years old are not open to the public, unless the subject is deceased. Copies of personnel and medical files for a federal employee can be requested by providing, in writing, the person's full name, date of birth, social security number (if known), name of agency where last employed, and the approximate date of employment. These records contain valuable genealogical information.

State Vital Statistics Offices

Where to Write for Birth, Marriage, and Death records

ALABAMA. Vital Records, Department of Public Health, Center for Health Statistics, PO Box 5625, Montgomery, AL 36103. Births and deaths since January, 1908, marriages since August, 1936. Fee for certified copy: $12.00.

ALASKA. Bureau of Vital Statistics, PO Box 110675, Juneau, AK 99811. Births, marriages, and deaths since January, 1913. Fee for certified copies: $10.00.

ARIZONA. Vital Records Section, Department of Health Services, PO Box 3887, Phoenix, AZ 85030. Births since 1884, deaths since 1887. Fee for certified copies: births, $9.00, deaths $6.00. Marriage records (and any births and deaths before statewide registration) are maintained by the Clerk of the Superior Court in each county.

ARKANSAS. Division of Vital Records, State Health Department, 4815 W. Markham St. S lot 44, Little Rock, AR 72205. Births and deaths since February, 1914, marriages since January, 1917. Fee for certified copies: births and marriages, $5.00; deaths, $4.00.

CALIFORNIA. Office of State Registrar of Vital Statistics, Department of Health, PO Box 730241, Sacramento, CA 95814. Births, deaths, and marriages since July, 1905. Fee for certified copies: $15.00.

COLORADO. Vital Records Section, Dept. of Health, 4300 Cherry Creek Dr., S., Denver, CO 80222. Births since 1910, deaths since 1900.

Fee for certified copies: $12.00. Marriage records are maintained by the County Clerk for each county. The Vital Records Section has a statewide index to marriages, 1900-1939, and 1975 to present. For a $12.00 search fee, the staff will search the index for a marriage.

CONNECTICUT. Vital Records Section, Department of Health Services, 150 Washington St., Hartford, CT 06106. Births, deaths, and marriages since July, 1897. Fee for certified copies: births, $15.00, deaths and marriages, $5.00.

DELAWARE. Office of Vital Statistics, Division of Public Health, PO Box 637, Dover, DE 19903. Births since 1921, deaths and marriages since 1953. Fee for certified copies: $6.00.

DISTRICT OF COLUMBIA. Vital Records Branch, Department of Human Services, 800 9th St., S.W., 1st Floor, Washington, DC 20024. Births and deaths since August, 1874. Fee for certified copies: births, $18.00, deaths, $12.00. Marriage records maintained by the Clerk of the District of Columbia Superior Court.

FLORIDA. Vital Statistics, Department of Health and Rehabilitative Services, PO box 210, Jacksonville, FL 32231. Births since 1917 (incomplete 1865-1916), deaths since 1917 (incomplete 1877-1916), and marriages since 1927. Fee for certified copies: births, $9.00; deaths and marriages, $5.00.

GEORGIA. Vital Records Service, Department of Human Resources, Room 217-H, 47 Trinity Ave. S.W., Atlanta, GA 30334. Births and deaths since January, 1919, marriages since Jun 1952. Fee for certified copies: $10.00.

HAWAII. Office of Health Status Monitoring, State Department of Health, PO Box 3378, Honolulu, HI 96801. Births, deaths, and marriages since 1853. Fee for certified copies: $2.00.

IDAHO. Vital Statistics Unit, Center for Vital Statistics and Health Policy, 450 W. State St., 1st Floor, PO Box 83720, Boise, ID 83720. Births and deaths since July, 1911, marriages since May, 1947. Fee for certified copies: $8.00.

ILLINOIS. Division of Vital Records, Department of Public Health, 605 W. Jefferson St., Springfield, IL 62702. Births and deaths since January, 1916, marriages since January, 1962. Fee for certified copies: births and deaths, $15.00; marriages, $5.00.

INDIANA. Vital Records Section, Indiana State Department of Health, 1330 W. Michigan St., PO Box 7125, Indianapolis, IN 46206. Births since October, 1907, deaths since January, 1900. Fee for certified copies: births, $6.00; deaths, $4.00. Marriage records are maintained by the County Clerk in each county.

IOWA. Vital Records, Department of Public Health, Lucas State Office Building, Des Moines, IA 50319. Births, deaths, and marriages since July, 1911 (incomplete from July, 1880). Fee for certified copies: $10.00.

KANSAS. Office of Vital Statistics, Department of Health and Environment, 900 S. Jackson, 1st floor, Room 151, Topeka, KS 66612. Births and deaths since July, 1911,

marriages since May, 1913. Fee for certified copies: births, $10.00; deaths and marriages, $7.00.

KENTUCKY. Office of Vital Statistics, Department for Health Services, 275 E. Main St., Frankfort, KY 40621. Births and deaths since January, 1911, marriages since January, 1958. Fee for certified copies: births, $9.00; deaths and marriages, $6.00.

LOUISIANA. Vital Records Registry, Department of Public Health, 325 Loyola Ave., New Orleans, LA 70112. Births, deaths, and marriages since July, 1914, New Orleans since 1892. Fee for certified copies: births, $13.00; deaths and marriages, $5.00. Older records available for $5.00 through Louisiana State Archives, PO Box 94125, Baton Rouge, LA 70804.

MAINE. Office of Vital Statistics, Department of Human Services, State House, Station 11, Augusta, ME 04333. Births, deaths, and marriages since January, 1923. Fee for certified copies: $10.00. Records 1892-1922 available at Maine State Archives, State House Station #84, Augusta, ME 04333-0084.

MARYLAND. Division of Vital Records, Department of Health and Mental Hygiene, PO Box 68760, Baltimore, MD 21215. Births and deaths since August, 1898, marriages since June, 1951. Fee for certified copies: $4.00.

MASSACHUSETTS. Registry of Vital Records and Statistics, 470 Atlantic Ave., 2nd Floor, Boston, MA 02210. Births, marriages, and deaths since January, 1901. Fee for certified copies: $11.00 by mail, $6.00 in person. Older records available for $4.00 from Massachusetts Archives, Columbia Point, 220 Morrissey Blvd., Boston, MA 02125.

MICHIGAN. Department of Community Health, Office of the State Registrar, 3423 Martin Luther King Jr. Blvd., PO Box 30195 Lansing, MI 48909. Births since 1893, deaths since 1897. Fee for certified copies: $13.00. Marriages from about 1867 available from County Clerk in each county.

MINNESOTA. Section of Vital Statistics Registration, Department of Health, PO Box 9441, Minneapolis, MN 55440. Births since January, 1900, deaths since January, 1908, and marriages since 1958. Fee for certified copies: births: births, $11.00; deaths and marriages, $8.00. Marriages before 1958 are maintained by the Clerk of the District Court in each county.

MISSISSIPPI. Vital Records Office, State Department of Health, 2423 N. State St., Jackson, MS 39216. Births and deaths since November, 1912, marriages from January 1926, to June, 1938 and since January, 1942. Fee for certified copies: births, $12.00; deaths and marriages, $10.00.

MISSOURI. Bureau of Vital Records, Department of Health, PO Box 570, Jefferson City, MO 65102. Births and deaths since January, 1910. Fee for certified copies: $10.00. Marriages maintained by the County Recorder of Deeds in each county. (Vital Records office will search their index to statewide marriage records from July, 1948 for no fee).

MONTANA. Bureau of Vital Records and Health Statistics, Department of Health and Human Services, Helena, MT 59620. Births and deaths since 1907. Fee for certified copies: $10.00. Marriages maintained by the County Clerk in each county.

NEBRASKA. Bureau of Vital Statistics, State Department of Health, PO Box 95007, Lincoln, NE 68509. Births and deaths since January, 1904, marriages since January, 1909. Fee for certified copies: births, $10.00; marriages and deaths, $9.00.

NEVADA. Division of Health, Vital Statistics, 505 E. King St., Room 102, Carson City, NV 89710. Births and deaths since July, 1911. Fee for certified copies: births, $11.00; deaths, $8.00. Marriage records maintained by County Recorder in each county. Vital Statistics Office has an index to statewide marriages since 1968.

NEW HAMPSHIRE. Bureau of Vital Records, Health and Welfare Building, 6 Hazen Dr., Concord, NH 03301. Births, marriages, and deaths since 1640 (earliest records incomplete). Fee for certified copies: $10.00.

NEW JERSEY. State Department of Health, Bureau of Vital Statistics, S. Warren and Market Sts., CN-370, Trenton, NJ 08625. Births, marriages, and deaths since June, 1878. Fee for certified copies: $4.00. Records 1848-1878 at NJ State Archives, Trenton, NJ 08625.

NEW MEXICO. Vital Statistics, New Mexico Health Services Division, PO Box 26110, Santa Fe, NM 87502. Births and deaths since 1889. (Date of earliest records varies from county to county). Fee for certified copies: births, $10.00; deaths, $5.00. Marriage records are maintained by the county clerk in each county.

NEW YORK (Except New York City). Vital Records Section, Department of Health, Corning Tower, Empire State Plaza, Albany, NY 12237. Births, deaths, and marriages since 1880. Fee for certified copies: births and deaths, $15.00; marriages, $5.00. (Contact registrar of Vital Statistics for the cities of Albany, Buffalo, and Yonkers who have births and deaths from 1914).

NEW YORK CITY. Division of Vital Records, Department of Health, 125 Worth St., Room 133, New York, NY 10013. Births since January, 1910, deaths since January, 1949. Fee for certified copies: $15.00. Marriages maintained by City Clerk, each borough. Older records at Archives Division, Department of Records and Information Services, 31 Chambers St., New York, NY 10007.

NORTH CAROLINA. North Carolina Vital Records, Vital Records Section, PO Box 29537, Raleigh, NC 27626. Births since October, 1913, deaths since January, 1946, marriages since January, 1962. Fee for certified copies: $10.00. Death records 1913 - 1945 at Archives and Records Section, 109 E. Jones St., Raleigh, NC 27611.

NORTH DAKOTA. Division of Vital Records, State Capitol, 600 E. Boulevard Ave., Bismarck, ND 58505. Births and deaths since 1923 (incomplete from 1893), marriages since July, 1925. Fee for certified copies: births, $7.00; deaths and marriages, $5.00.

OHIO. Bureau of Vital Statistics, Department of Health, PO Box 15098, Columbus, OH 43215. Births since December, 1908, deaths since January, 1937. Fee for certified copies: $7.00 (non-certified copy: $1.10). Marriage records are maintained by the Probate Judge in each county. Original death records 1908 - 1936 are located at the Ohio Historical Society, Archives Library Division, 1985 Velma Ave., Columbus, OH 43211.

OKLAHOMA. Vital Records Section, State Department of Health, PO Box 53551, Oklahoma City, OK 73152. Births and deaths since October, 1908. Fee for certified copies: births, $5.00; deaths, $10.00. Marriage records

are maintained the Clerk of Court in each county.

OREGON. Vital Statistics Section, Health Division, Department of Human Resources, PO Box 14050, Portland, OR 97293. Births and deaths since January, 1903, marriages since January, 1906. Fee for certified copies: $13.00. (For $1.00 and a SASE, photocopies of original death certificates, 1903-1940, can be obtained from the Oregon State Archives, 1005 Broadway, NE, Salem, OR 97310).

PENNSYLVANIA. Division of Vital Records, Department of Health, PO Box 1528, New Castle, PA 16103. Births and deaths since January, 1906. Fee for certified copies: births, $4.00, deaths, $3.00. Marriages records can be obtained from the Marriage License Clerk in each county courthouse.

RHODE ISLAND. Division of Vital Records, Department of Health, 3 Capitol Hill, Room 101, Providence, RI 02908. Births for the past 100 years and deaths for the past 50 years, and marriages since 1853. Fee for certified copies: $15.00. For earlier records, write to the city/town clerk where the event occurred or to the Rhode Island State Archives, 337 Westminster Street, Providence, RI 02903.

SOUTH CAROLINA. Office of Vital Records and Public Health Statistics, Department of Health and Environmental Control, 2600 Bull St., Columbia, SC 29201. Births and deaths since January, 1915, marriages since July, 1950. Fee for certified copies: $8.00.

SOUTH DAKOTA. Vital Records, Department of Health, 445 E. Capitol, Pierre, SD 57501. Births, deaths, and marriages since July, 1905. Fee for certified copies: $7.00.

TENNESSEE. Vital Records, Department of Health, TN Tower, 3rd Floor, 312 8th Ave., N., Nashville, TN 37247. Births and deaths since January, 1914, marriages since July, 1945. Fee for certified copies: births and marriages, $10.00; deaths, $5.00.

TEXAS. Bureau of Vital Statistics, Department of Health, PO Box 12040, Austin, TX 78711. Births and deaths since January, 1903 (incomplete for 1903 to 1909). Fee for certified copies: births, $11.00, deaths; $9.00. Marriage records are maintained by the County Clerk in each county.

UTAH. Bureau of Vital Records, Utah Department of Health, PO Box 142855, Salt Lake City, UT 84114. Births and deaths since January, 1905, marriages since 1978. Fee for certified copies: births, $12.00; deaths and marriages, $9.00.

VERMONT. Vital Records Section, Department of Health, PO Box 70, Burlington, VT 05402. Births, deaths, and marriages for the past 100 years. Fee for certified copies:, $5.00. Earlier records back to 1760 are at General Services Center, Public Records Division, Drawer 32, U.S. Rte 2 - Middlesex, Montpelier, VT 05633.

VIRGINIA. Division of Vital Records, Department of Health, PO Box 1000, Richmond, VA 23208. Births, deaths, and marriages since January, 1853 (incomplete 1896-1912). Fee for certified copies: $8.00.

WASHINGTON. Center for Health Statistics, Department of Health, PO Box 9709, Olympia, WA 98507. Births and deaths since July, 1907, marriages since January, 1968. Fee for certified copies: $11.00.

WEST VIRGINIA. Vital Registration Office, Division of Health, Capitol Complex, Building 3, Charleston, WV 25305. Births and deaths since 1917, marriages since January, 1921. Fee for certified copies: $5.00.

WISCONSIN. Vital Records, 1 West Wilson St., Madison, WI 53701. Births, deaths, and marriages since January, 1907 (incomplete records as early as 1814). Fee for certified copies: births, $10.00; deaths and marriages, $7.00.

WYOMING. Vital Records Services, Hathaway Building, Cheyenne, WY 82002. Births and deaths since July, 1909, marriages since May, 1941. Fee for certified copies: births and marriages, $11.00; deaths, $9.00.